Excavations
at the Indian Creek Site,
Antigua, West Indies

Excavations at the Indian Creek Site, Antigua, West Indies

Irving Rouse
Birgit Faber Morse

With an appendix by
Elizabeth S. Wing

YALE UNIVERSITY PUBLICATIONS IN ANTHROPOLOGY
NUMBER EIGHTY-TWO 1999
Department of Anthropology, Yale University
Division of Anthropology,
Peabody Museum of Natural History
New Haven, Connecticut

Yale University Publications in Anthropology

Curatorial Editor-in-Chief
Frank Hole

Executive Editor
Lawrence F. Gall

Publications Editor
Rosemary Volpe

The *Yale University Publications in Anthropology* series embodies the results of researches in the general field of anthropology directly conducted or sponsored by the University Department of Anthropology and the Yale Peabody Museum Division of Anthropology. Occasionally, other manuscripts of outstanding quality that deal with subjects of special interest to the Faculty of the Departments of Anthropology may also be included. Issues range in size from brief papers to extensive monographs and are numbered consecutively as independent contributions and appear at irregular intervals.

Titles in the YUPA series may be obtained through the Yale Peabody Museum Publications Office. For information see our website at http://www.peabody.yale.edu /publications, or address inquiries to:

Publications Office
Peabody Museum of Natural History
Yale University
170 Whitney Avenue
P.O. Box 208118
New Haven, CT 06520-8118 U.S.A.

Cover illustration: Wor ware modeled head lug in the Indian Creek style.
© 1999 Armand Morgan.

ISBN: 0-913516-19-8
Printed in the U.S.A.

♾ This paper meets the requirements of ANSI/NISO Z39.48-1992 (Permanence of Paper).

CONTENTS

List of Figures

List of Tables

PREFACE

In 1973 the Antigua Historical Society hosted the Fifth International Congress for the Study of Pre-Columbian Cultures of the Lesser Antilles. Desiring to increase the number of local artifacts available for display at the Congress, the Society invited Irving Rouse to excavate just beforehand at the recently discovered site of Indian Creek. Already fully committed to other research, he at first refused, but was persuaded to accept with the understanding that he would be unable to prepare a final report for at least 10 years. That 10 years has stretched to 25, and the research of colleagues has suffered from having to rely on Rouse's increasingly obsolete preliminary reports (1974, 1976, 1978). Professor Rouse wishes to express his regrets for the delay.

The invitation to excavate at Indian Creek was attractive because it offered the opportunity to fill a gap in the regional chronology that Rouse had established for the Lesser Antilles (Rouse 1964, Fig. 4). The aim was to formulate a sequence of local periods for the island of Antigua and to use this sequence to test the conflicting hypotheses on the migration of Ceramic Age peoples from South America into the West Indies. Rouse's preliminary reports were devoted to these tasks.

Thanks to the subsequent research of our colleagues, especially Petersen (1996), Petersen and Watters (1999) on Montserrat, S. M. Wilson (unpublished data from *Prehistory of Nevis,* manuscript in the Department of Anthropology, University of Texas, Austin, Texas) on Nevis, Versteeg and Schinkel (1992) on St. Eustatius, and Hofman and Hoogland (1993) on Saba, we have been able to proceed a step further in the present report. Not only have we refined Rouse's original sequence of Antiguan periods, but we have also combined it with the sequences that have since become available for the other Leeward Islands to produce the first comprehensive regional chronology. We have used that chronology to make a more conclusive test of the migration hypotheses.

In the years since Rouse published his preliminary reports, West Indian archaeologists have expanded the scope of their research from cultural history, which was his primary concern, to cultural ecology and cognition, and have introduced the methods appropriate to those recently developed subdisciplines. Our Indian Creek research is designed to contribute only to cultural history. Nevertheless, we hope that our results will also be of use to those interested in ecology and cognition, if only as a framework within which to draw their conclusions.

The Indian Creek excavations were sponsored jointly by the Antigua Archaeological Society, by Yale University's Department of Anthropology, and by the Division of Anthropology at the Yale Peabody Museum of Natural History. Rouse planned and directed the fieldwork until he had to be hospitalized with heat exhaustion while digging the fifth of six excavations. A partnership consisting of Desmond Nicholson, president of the Society, Fred Olsen, its secretary-treasurer, and Egbert J. H. Boestra, the government archaeologist from Aruba who had come to observe the fieldwork, completed the work. Professor Rouse wishes to express his appreciation to them.

We are indebted to Dave Davis, then an anthropology student in the Yale Graduate School of Arts and Sciences, for taking the time from his own excavations at Jolly Beach to map the Indian Creek site. Desmond Nicholson of the Antigua National Museum has helped us in many ways, especially during our return trip to Antigua in 1993 when he supplied us with information about the most recent work at Indian Creek. William K. Sacco at Yale University photographed the artifacts. Armand Morgan at Yale's Peabody Museum of Natural History drew the illustrations. Rouse's excavations were supported by matching grants from friends of the Antigua Archaeological Society and the National Science Foundation (No. GS-37970). We thank Elizabeth Olsen Kyburg for defraying the costs of publication.

Irving Rouse
Birgit Faber Morse
Department of Anthropology
Yale University
New Haven, Connecticut
January 1999

CHAPTER ONE

INTRODUCTION

Geographical Setting

Antigua Island is centrally situated on the Guadeloupe Passage, which separates the southern half of the Lesser Antilles, known as the Windward Islands, from the northern half, known as the Leeward Islands (Figure 1). Guadeloupe Island forms the southern side of the passage. Antigua is at the Atlantic end of the northern side, with Montserrat at the Caribbean end. Christopher Columbus landed on Guadeloupe Island during his second voyage, but modern mariners prefer to head for Antigua since it is on the shortest direct route between Europe and the West Indies. Montserrat would have provided the first native settlers, who came from South America, with a better route northwards because it is closer to Guadeloupe.

Montserrat and Antigua have very different environments. Montserrat is a small, high volcanic island. Its cones attract heavy rainfall that feeds large streams and supports luxuriant tropical vegetation. Antigua is larger and has extensive sedimentary deposits. Rain clouds pass over its mountains, only half the height of Montserrat's, without dropping their moisture; as a result Antigua cannot support large streams and lush vegetation (W. M. Davis 1926:45–8, 144–65). Montserrat's environment extends northward along the Caribbean side of the Leeward archipelago through Nevis, St. Kitts and St. Eustatius to Saba, all of which are also small, high volcanic islands. Antigua's environmental conditions continue north along the Atlantic side to Barbuda, where they are more extreme; that island is nearly flat and completely sedimentary.

The dichotomy between the Caribbean and Atlantic islands gives way farther north to a third cluster dominated by St. Bartholémy, St. Martin and Anguilla. While they, too, are small, their relatively low altitude makes them more similar in environment to Antigua (W. M. Davis 1926:166–9). Beyond them, the broad Anegada Passage separates the Leewards from the Virgin Islands and the rest of the Greater Antilles. Taken together the southwestern arc of high volcanic islands and the northern group of relatively low islands provide the best route from the Windwards through the Leewards into the Greater Antilles. Antigua and Barbuda lead out into the Atlantic Ocean.

South of Guadeloupe Passage, the Windwards consist of a single chain of large

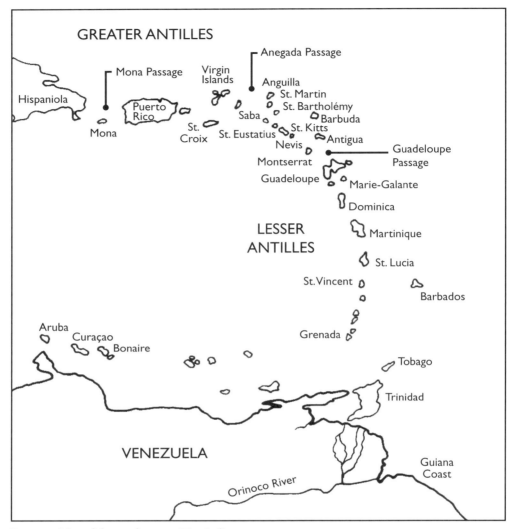

FIGURE 1. Map of the northeastern West Indies.

mountainous islands extending from Guadeloupe through Dominica, Martinique, St. Lucia, St. Vincent and the Grenadines to Grenada. A relatively broad expanse of sea separates Grenada from the South American coastal islands of Tobago and Trinidad. The Windwards also include the isolated island of Barbados in the Atlantic Ocean some distance east of St. Vincent. Barbados bears the same relationship to the rest of the Windwards that Barbuda does to the rest of the Leewards, but is farther removed from the main chain. It was therefore much more difficult for the native West Indians to reach, especially since the prevailing winds and currents impede travel from St. Vincent to Barbados. The trade winds have little effect on navigation within the Leeward Islands because they blow from the northeast across that island chain. There is one exception: travelers from Montserrat to Antigua must head into these trade winds.

The South Equatorial current, augmented by an enormous outpouring of water from the mouth of the Orinoco River, favors movement from south to north, including travel from Guadeloupe to Montserrat and the other volcanic islands on the Caribbean side of the Leeward chain, and from Guadeloupe through Antigua to Barbuda on the Atlantic side.

Ethnohistorical Background

Crossing the Atlantic Ocean for the second time, in November 1493 Columbus landed on Guadeloupe's satellite island of Marie-Galante. Proceeding to the main island (Figure 1), he then sailed north along the Caribbean side of the Leewards, naming each island except Barbuda, which was off his course. Anxious to go to the relief of the sailors left behind in Haiti after their ship had been wrecked there during his first voyage, he did not stop anywhere.

The accounts of the parties sent ashore on Marie-Galante and Guadeloupe indicate that the inhabitants of those islands were Island-Caribs. They fled from their villages as the Spaniards approached, leaving behind partially consumed human flesh and captives seized during raids on Taino villages in the Greater Antilles. Columbus took the captives back to their homes (Morison 1942, 1:67–72).

The Spanish settlers paid relatively little attention to the Lesser Antilles, at first preoccupied with colonization of the Greater Antilles and then drawn to the mainland by the wealth to be gained by plundering the civilized peoples of Mexico and Peru. Other than an abortive attempt by Antonio Serrano to settle Antigua in 1520 (Flannigan 1844, 1:3), the conquistadors used the Leeward Islands only as a source of supplies when traveling between colonies in the Greater Antilles and South America, and for slaves to replace the Tainos, decimated by being forced to work on plantations and in mines. There was also a reverse movement of Tainos fleeing to the Leewards from the Spanish colonies in Puerto Rico and Hispaniola (Rouse 1992:155–8). The buccaneers who preyed on the Spanish empire also came to the Leewards for supplies (Harris 1965:79–83). The Island-Caribs used the archipelago as a base from which to attack the Spanish settlements in the Greater Antilles. The Spaniards avoided the Windward Islands because of the Island-Caribs' ability to defend themselves, preferring to proceed directly from the Leewards to their colonies in South America.

From the time of Columbus' visit to the Lesser Antilles in 1493 until the beginning of colonization in 1632, the native inhabitants of both the Leeward and Windward Islands may be said to have lived in a Protohistoric Age. In the absence of adequate documentation for this age, our information about it must come primarily from the study of its remains. Unfortunately, local archaeologists have been preoccupied with the early Ceramic Age Saladoid migration that introduced agriculture and pottery, and have paid relatively little attention to either the late Ceramic or the Pro-

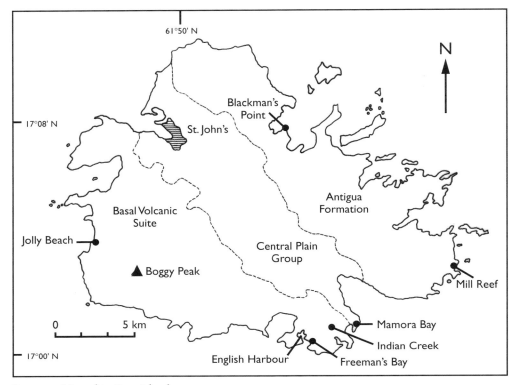

FIGURE 2. Map of Antigua Island.

tohistoric Ages. We still do not know, for example, to what extent the Leewards were depopulated by Island-Carib and Spanish raids.

Many authorities have assumed that the late Ceramic Age Island-Caribs had established an outpost at Salt River on St. Croix, the largest of the Virgin Islands, because the party Columbus set ashore there during his second voyage was attacked by hostile Indians. However, extensive excavation at Salt River by Hatt (1924) and Vescelius (1952) has shown that the final aboriginal inhabitants of that site were Taino Indians. Evidently the Spaniards misidentified them as Caribs because, in their need to defend themselves against Island-Carib raids, they had become more war-like than their relatives farther west (Rouse 1992:146–7; Morse 1997).

Study of the distribution of the Island-Caribs was for a long time hampered by a lack of knowledge about the nature of their pottery. Louis Allaire (1994) has now been able to identify it, assigning it to a ceramic series in the Windward Islands known as Cayoid. Since no Cayoid pottery has been found in either the Virgin or the Leeward Islands, we must conclude that the Island-Caribs did not establish permanent settlements there during either the late Ceramic Age or the Protohistoric Age.

Who, then, did live in the Leewards during this time? Recent archaeological research, to be discussed in the conclusion to this monograph, has extended the late Ceramic Age distribution of the Tainos southward from the Virgin Islands into the northern Leewards. It has further shown that the southwestern and southeastern Leeward Islands were then inhabited by peoples related to the predecessors of the Island-Caribs in the Windward Islands. Consequently, the term *Igneri,* which the Island-Caribs applied to their predecessors, may appropriately be extended to the population of the southwestern and southeastern Leewards in the time of Columbus (Rouse et al. 1995). It is uncertain how long the Tainos and the Igneris survived in their respective parts of the Leeward Islands. They were certainly gone by the end of the Protohistoric Age; the first European colonists found the Leewards uninhabited (Harris 1965:84–5).

The Island of Antigua

Antigua is roughly circular in shape, circa 21 by 19 km with an area of 280 sq km. It is located at 17° to 17°10′ north latitude and 61°40′ to 61°55′ west longitude. The geology of Antigua dates back to the early Oligocene, over 30 million years ago, and includes a history of volcanism and later, after the decline of volcanic activity, an accumulation of shallow water marine and littoral deposits. Some of these deposits have been exposed by relative changes in sea level associated with tilting and faulting (Martin-Kaye 1959).

Geologically and physiographically Antigua can be divided into three distinct regions trending from northwest to southeast: a southwestern volcanic region, a central plain and a northeastern limestone area (Figure 2).

The southwestern region is an area of high hills, deeply incised valleys and steep-sided slopes consisting of eroded remnants of the volcano that formed the island. Called the Basal Volcanic Suite (Multer et al. 1986; Weiss 1994), these are composed mostly of eruptive tuffs and agglomerates, as well as basalt and andesite. Boggy Peak, the highest point on the island, rises circa 400 m above sea level.

The central plain is a broad, low valley trending roughly northeast to southeast that does not rise above 17 m except for an occasional feature. The valley is floored with a mixture of marine and nonmarine sediments and reworked volcanic materials called the Central Plain Group. It is farmed extensively.

The northeastern limestone area rises from the low central plain to about 100 m above sea level. It consists of emerged limestone and reef components. The underlying rock, called the Antigua Formation, consists predominately of reworked siliceous volcanics (Weiss 1994). This upland is drained by mature river valleys and streams that originate at the center of the island and run northeast. Its coast is indented with a number of sand- and mangrove-fringed bays bordered by many islands.

Antigua's tropical climate is modified by the effect of the surrounding ocean. The climate tends towards the extremes, varying between long, dry spells and short, wet periods, with mean maximum and minimum temperatures of 83°F (29°C) and 73°F (23°C), respectively. The humidity ranges between 70% and 80% and is highest towards the end of the year. The island, however, is noted for its breezes and for the constant northeast trade winds, which are strongest during the early months and lessen the effect of the high humidity. The average yearly rainfall is only about 115 cm, half of which comes during the hurricane season from August to November. There is a marked dry season during the first months of the year.

The volcanic region, with the highest elevation and the steepest slopes, has the greatest rainfall—up to 130 cm per year. The Indian Creek site is located here, close to the south shore and to the border with the central plains region. The plains, with their lower elevation and gentler topography, receive about 115 cm of rain annually. The limestone area on the Atlantic side of the island receives the least amount, only 100–105 cm (Multer et al. 1986). Reef communities with an abundance of marine organisms survive on the Atlantic coast adjacent to its many bays and islands. Most of the Antigua's preceramic sites have been discovered in this part of the island.

Antigua's low and markedly seasonal rainfall, with its great variability from year to year, may have been a major reason why the first precolumbian agriculturalists were slow to settle the island. The Europeans would have found the relatively sparse rainfall more attractive, and it may have been a factor in their decision to make Antigua the scene of their initial, abortive attempt to settle in the Leeward Islands.

CHAPTER TWO

THE INDIAN CREEK SITE

Location

The Indian Creek site is situated in the Parish of St. Paul in the southeastern corner of Antigua's volcanic region (Figure 2) and lies between two deep inlets, English Harbour to its west and Mamora Bay to its east. While both of these bodies of water support relatively large populations, the site is in open country, a fact that has contributed to its preservation. The Indian Creek site takes its name from a dried up streambed that empties into a small rocky cove. According to our workers at the site, the stream was active until construction of the road from English Harbour to Mamora Bay cut it off from its catchment area. The site is 800 m upstream from the cove, in a natural amphitheater separated from the sea to its south by low hills, from English Harbour to its west by a much broader range of higher hills, and from Mamora Bay to its east by a narrower and lower range. This is unusual; most Antiguan sites are within sight of the sea.

The closest sites are Freeman's Bay, to the west at the entrance to English Harbour, and Mamora Bay, to the east on the far shore of that bay (Figure 2). These two sites are in more normal positions, Freeman's Bay on a sandy beach and Mamora Bay on high ground close to the shore. Steep cliffs rising directly from the sea separate the Freeman's Bay site from Indian Creek (Harris 1965, Fig. 3). The hills between the Indian Creek and the Mamora Bay sites are lower and the shoreline is easier to traverse. Consequently the inhabitants of the Indian Creek site must have been able to interact more closely with their neighbors on Mamora Bay.

History

In July 1956, Fisheries officer Ralph Camacho reported the presence of shells alongside the Indian Creek to Dr. Fred Olsen, a chemical engineer who had led a group of amateur archaeologists in excavating at the Mill Reef site farther east along the coast (Figure 2). Olsen visited the scene of the new discovery and found that it was indeed a place of habitation. Impressed by its location, by the state of its preservation and by the quality of its artifacts, he decided to seek professional advice. In January 1959 he

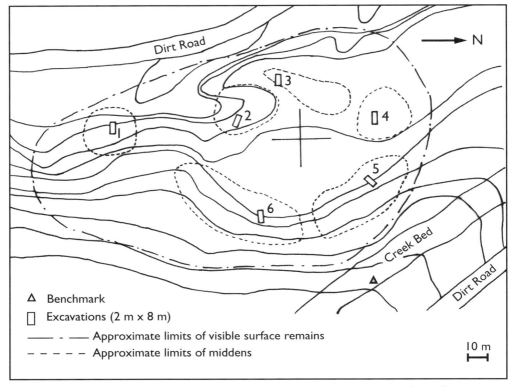

FIGURE 3. Map of the Indian Creek site showing Excavations 1 through 6. Contour interval is 1 m.

showed it to Rouse, who agreed that it had great potentiality and recommended that it be left untouched until arrangements could be made for excavation by a fully qualified person. When Charles A. Hoffman, Jr. made an archaeological survey of the island in 1961, he found traces of human occupation on the rocky shore at the mouth of the Indian Creek. He did not go upstream to search for the source of these remains. On May 19, 1969 Desmond V. Nicholson and author Carleton Mitchell noticed that recent rains had washed artifacts out of a deep gully in the richest part of the site. They dug a test pit there, dividing it into five levels, and displayed their finds in the Dockyard Museum at English Harbour (Mitchell 1971:121).

Joining forces under the sponsorship of the Antigua Archaeological Society, Olsen and Nicholson then sought to arrange for excavation of the site. Over the next four years they raised a large sum of money for the purpose from friends and associates in the Society. They set a date of spring 1973 for the work to be done, timing it to take place just before the opening of the Fifth International Congress for the Study of Pre-Columbian Cultures of the Lesser Antilles in St. Johns, Antigua, in order to be able to display the finds there.

They asked Rouse to conduct the excavations. He declined, pleading the pressure of other obligations, but finally accepted with the understanding that he would not be able to write a final report on the work until he had completed his previous commitments. (His estimate of a delay of 10 years has grown to 25.) Rouse obtained a matching grant from the National Science Foundation (No. GS-37970) and commenced work on May 28, 1973. He continued until June 25, when he fell ill and had to be hospitalized. His illness was misdiagnosed as a heart attack and, after receiving treatment, Rouse was shipped directly home without being able to participate in the rest of the fieldwork or in the congress. His Yale doctors found that he had suffered from heat exhaustion, presumably caused in part by overwork trying to prepare exhibits for the congress while excavating full-time, and in part by conditions in the building where he had been setting up the exhibits. A former U.S. tracking station built without windows, its air conditioning equipment had been removed by the U.S. government when the building was given to the government of Antigua, leaving it without adequate ventilation.

In Rouse's absence, Olsen and Nicholson took charge of the excavations at Indian Creek and continued according to Rouse's plan with the assistance of Egbert H. J. Boestra, a Dutch archaeologist who had come from Aruba to observe the work. They finished Excavation 5 and dug all of Excavation 6, completing it on July 13. In the nine days left before the beginning of the congress they chose to dig an additional trench at the lower end of Excavation 6 and perpendicular to it. This trench consisted of six 2 sq m sections, the first four of which were designated Excavation 7 and the last two Excavation 8. These two excavations are not shown in Figure 3 because they were not part of this research. They were intended to sample what appeared to be the richest part of the site and to provide the Antigua Archaeological Society with a representative collection. That collection became the nucleus for the present Museum of Antigua and Barbuda.

Rouse returned to Antigua during the following Christmas and New Year holidays to check on what had been done. While there, he also dug briefly at the Freeman's Bay site in an effort to complete the sequence of periods he had found at Indian Creek (Rouse et al. 1995).

One other set of systematic excavations has been undertaken at Indian Creek. In December 1977, January 1978 and August 1979 Alick R. Jones (1980a, 1980b, 1985) trowelled five small columns into the walls of Yale Excavations 4, 5 and 6 to obtain more complete samples of food remains. Taken together, his study of the ecofacts and this study of the artifacts provide a complete picture of the changes in culture that took place at the site. Additionally, shortly after the end of Rouse's fieldwork, amateur archaeologist Ogden D. Starr (unpublished data from *Excavations at Indian Creek, Antigua,* manuscript in the Museum of Antigua and Barbados, St. John's, Antigua) and Dave Davis, who had mapped the site for Rouse, dug test pits in the richest deposits near Excavation 6. Otherwise, the site has remained in unusually pristine condition.

Description

After several years of drought in the 1960s, the Indian Creek site was almost bare of vegetation; only a few acacia shrubs (which today form a dense thicket) could be seen. Large amounts of conch and other shells were visible around the edge of the site, pro-

FIGURE 4. Aerial photograph of the Indian Creek site, looking south. The bed of the creek is marked by the band of trees in the center of the picture, ending in the estuary on the inner bay. Photograph courtesy of the Fred Olsen Trust.

viding evidence of prehistoric occupation, along with specimens of petrified wood scattered over the ground, showing that trees once grew in this part of Antigua. (Traces of a petrified forest have been found at Corbinson Point on the south coast, including a 90 cm wide stump and long spreading roots in the lava deposits that underlie beds of Oligocene limestone laid down millions of years ago.) Besides the shells left by the precolumbian settlers and the remnants of petrified trees, the ground at Indian Creek was also littered with debris from the surrounding limestone beds (Olsen 1974).

From the air, the site, which covers more than eight hectares (20 acres), has the appearance of an oval ring, with a light grey color against a darker background. At ground level one can see that the grey color is due to the concentration of shell refuse in a series of middens that extends around the periphery of an oval area measuring circa 280 m by 165 m (Rouse 1974). Refuse seems to be sparse inside this oval area. It is a strong possibility that what little was there has been eroded downhill since the site was cleared and plowed for growing cotton during colonial times.

Rouse (1974) was able to identify six middens (Figure 3). The four (Middens 1–4) on the uphill side of the site are considerably smaller and shallower than the two (Middens 5 and 6) on the downhill side. Two gullies in the southernmost uphill midden showed that its height is only about 50 cm. A gully in the longer of the two downhill middens (Midden 6) revealed a height of almost 2 m. Many artifacts have been collected by local people from these open gullies, indicating that the downhill middens were considerably richer in material than the uphill ones.

Excavations

The gently sloping plateau on which the site is situated narrows towards the south where the now dry Indian Creek passed through an opening in the hills on the way to the coast. To the north the slope broadens into a large flat area, which would have been suitable for growing crops.

Rouse originally assumed that the inhabitants of Indian Creek had lived around the edge of the plateau and had formed the ring of middens by depositing their refuse where they lived. He thought that the area within the ring was an open plaza (Rouse 1974:167). Recent settlement pattern studies by Peter Siegel (1992) at Maisabel in Puerto Rico and by Aad Versteeg and Kees Schinkel (1992) at the Golden Rock site on St. Eustatius have led us to rethink these assumptions. We now hypothesize that the people who lived at Indian Creek built their houses in the so-called plaza area and threw their refuse around the periphery of their village. If correct, excavation in the plaza area should yield traces of structures, except possibly in the very center of the site where there may have been a much smaller plaza (Rouse and Morse 1999).

Had Rouse been aware of this interpretation while digging the site, it would not have affected his procedure. He chose to concentrate on the peripheral ring of middens because it was the only place to obtain the pottery needed to establish a sequence of periods of occupation.

Middens 5 and 6 would have been the obvious places to begin excavating since

A. Excavation 1

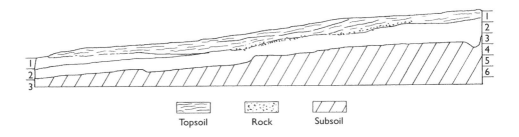

B. Excavation 2

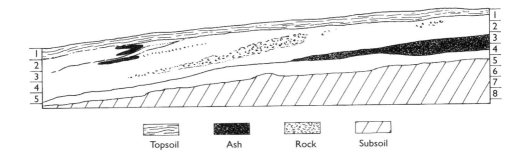

C. Excavation 3

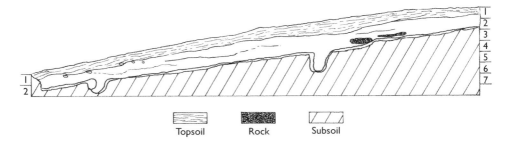

FIGURE 5. Profiles of the south walls of Excavations 1 through 6, showing levels excavated at 25 cm intervals.

D. Excavation 4

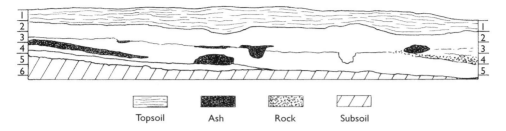

Topsoil   Ash   Rock   Subsoil

E. Excavation 5

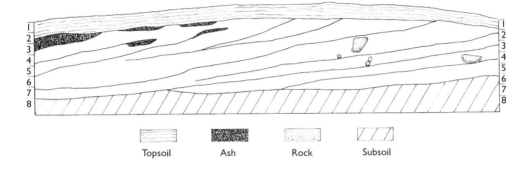

Topsoil   Ash   Rock   Subsoil

F. Excavation 6

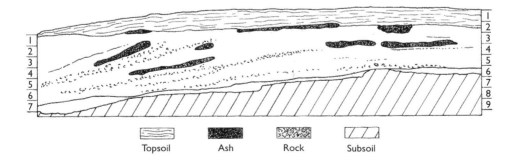

Topsoil   Ash   Rock   Subsoil

they were the deepest part of the ring and had yielded the most elaborate surface finds. However, these middens were not well suited to formulating a chronology as they had likely been disturbed by repeated episodes of erosion such as the one that had originally attracted attention to the site. Rouse therefore chose to start with Midden 1 and to proceed systematically around the ring, ending with Midden 6. In each midden, a trench was dug composed of four 2 sq m sections divided into artificial 25 cm levels. Unless impelled by other considerations, each trench was located in the highest part of its midden in an effort to obtain the maximum number of levels. Each trench was dug to the bottom of its refuse and then its floor was tested to make sure that there was no more refuse beneath it.

Two workers were assigned to each section, one to dig the refuse and the other to screen it. Picks and shovels were used except when dealing with perishable materials, which were removed with trowels and processed separately. The refuse was sifted through one-quarter inch mesh screens. This procedure was designed to recover as many artifacts as possible at the expense of the smaller ecofacts, that is, the unworked stone, flint and faunal remains not pertinent to the objective of establishing an artifactual chronology. Only samples of these were kept. Rouse encountered few features, such as layers, lenses or refuse pits, in the excavations he directed (Excavations 1–4 and the top of Excavation 5). He dug these features personally with a trowel and processed their contents separately. In his absence, this procedure does not seem to have been followed in the rest of Excavation 5 or in Excavation 6.

The collection from the Indian Creek site, then, consists of two kinds of assemblages of artifacts and ecofacts: those obtained from the arbitrary excavation units, each consisting of a single section and level; and those found in the few features distinguishable while digging the arbitrary units. Both kinds of assemblages have been used in the present study.

All bits of charcoal were collected, either from the trenches, in the screens or beneath them, and bagged separately according to the excavation unit or feature from which they came, so that each sample could be used to date the assemblage of artifacts and ecofacts with which it was found. The assemblages of artifacts and ecofacts were put into cloth bags and the assemblages of charcoal into plastic bags. Rouse took detailed notes on the composition of the refuse in each excavation unit. He also entered a description of each feature in his notes and drew a profile of one side wall in each excavation (Figure 5, A–F).

The following description of the excavations is limited to the six planned by Rouse. Excavations 7 and 8 are not discussed here since they were not part of the Yale-Antigua Archaeological Society project.

Excavation 1. The first midden to be dug was the smallest, shallowest and farthest away from the rich concentration of remains in Excavations 5 and 6. Nevertheless this midden had attracted attention because Desmond Nicholson (personal communication) found the first zoned incised crosshatched ("zic") sherds on its surface and Fred Olsen (1974, Fig. 4) collected three plain three-pointers of shell there. Indeed, it seems to be the only place in the site where evidence of the original settlers comes to the surface.

The top of the midden was flat, except in its southern part where water draining from the lowest point in a road along its uphill side had eroded two small gullies. Rouse chose to locate his excavation between the two gullies to recover the remains thus exposed before they, too, washed away. He numbered the four sections A1 to A4, proceeding uphill towards the road (Figure 5, A). Section A1 yielded refuse only through two 25 cm levels, and Sections A2–A4 through the top 5–12 cm of a third level.

The soil was predominantly dark brown, often flecked with bits of ash and charcoal. Occasional patches of light brown dirt, like that in the surrounding terrain, may have been deposited by erosion down the hillside. This kind of soil, in more compacted form, also underlay the deposit (Figure 5, A).

The refuse contained a moderate number of igneous rocks (some of which were fire cracked), pieces of coral and fossil wood, and fragments of flint. Crab jaws were the most prominent faunal feature, but animal bones and shells were rare. The top shell (*Cittarium pica*) was most noticeable, followed by conches (especially *Strombus gigas*) and olive shells (*Oliva* sp.). There were few bivalves. Land snails were ubiquitous in this excavation and the subsequent ones. Desmond Nicholson (personal communication) has suggested that they fed on the refuse.

A solid chunk of charcoal, possibly the remains of a log, was encountered 45–57 cm deep along the north side of Sections A1 and A2. A pit 57 cm in diameter extended down beneath the refuse in Section A2 from a depth of 62 cm to 78 cm (Figure 5, A). It was packed with turtle and manatee bones. Ribs and some teeth had been placed at its bottom and long bones had been stuffed in vertically above them.

The number of artifacts totals 2,560, of which 2,445 are ceramic, 105 lithic and 10 shell.

Excavation 2. The second trench was dug in the highest part of Midden 2, 72 m north of Excavation 1 and 8 m west of the north-south line in the center of the site (Figure 3). Its four sections, numbered C1 through C4, extended up a rather abrupt slope in a westerly direction. Presumably the inhabitants of the site lived at the base of this slope and heaped their refuse on it. Midden 2 was much deeper than Midden 1. Section 1 had to be dug through five 25 cm levels; Sections C2 and C3 halfway through the fifth level; and Section C4 through the fourth level. The decline in these depths indicates the trench was situated on the uphill side of the midden.

The soil was medium brown and friable. Ash and charcoal were scattered throughout and, in addition, there were three concentrations of ash, two of them well enough defined to be identified as distinct features (Figure 5, B). One was a pit 60 cm in diameter and the other a circular lense 38 cm long. No stones were found in either, but the second contained bits of charcoal. The subsoil was orange brown and more compact. We noted no traces of an appreciable lapse in the process of deposition, nor of erosion (Figure 6, top).

FIGURE 6. Excavations at the Indian Creek site. Irving Rouse with local workers and volunteers. Top, Excavation 2. Bottom, Excavation 3. Photographs courtesy of the Fred Olsen Trust.

Field stones and pieces of petrified wood were scattered throughout the deposit. Some showed signs of fire cracking. Fragments of flint were less common than in Excavation 1; the amount of coral was about the same. We encountered large rocks at the bottoms of Sections C2 and C4, one of which was too big to move. Elsewhere the subsoil had the appearance of disintegrating rock. It would seem, therefore, that the inhabitants were depositing their refuse on terrain unsuitable for cultivation.

Shells dominated over crab remains throughout all but the bottom level of this excavation and occurred in much greater variety, including as many bivalves as univalves. These proportions were reversed in the bottom level, where conditions were comparable to those in the previous excavation. Fish bones were relatively common throughout.

The number of artifacts totals 5,592, of which 5,385 are ceramic, 181 are lithic and 26 shell.

Excavation 3. The next trench was dug in a slight rise at the southern end of Midden 3 (Figure 3). It was 30 m northwest of Excavation 2 and 10 m south of the east-west line through the center of the site. This trench was begun at the eastern edge of the midden and extended westward through four sections designated E1 through E4. Refuse was found to a depth of 25 cm in the near half of Section E1, 38 cm in its far half, and 50 cm in Sections E2 through E4. The base of the refuse sloped appreciably upwards in all four sections, indicating that it had been deposited on a hillside, presumably by people who lived on the plateau in the central part of the site.

The soil was dark brown in color and quite dusty, especially at the far end of the trench where ash and charcoal were more common (Figure 5, C). The subsoil was yellowish brown and crumbly, but lacked the rocks found at the base of Midden 2. No pits, lenses or other features were observed (Figure 6, bottom).

Scattered through the deposit were field stones (many of them fire cracked), pieces of flint and fragments of coral. Both shells and the remains of crabs were less common than in the previous excavation. There was the same broad range of shells. The animal bones showed no appreciable differences.

The number of artifacts totals 1,964, of which 1,895 are ceramic, 55 lithic and 14 shell.

Excavation 4. While Midden 4 is at the same altitude as Midden 3, its greater height makes it the tallest point in the site. From it one has an uninterrupted view southward to the row of hills bordering the sea, westward across the creek to the range that separates the site from Mamora Bay, and northward to the road at the head of the creek.

Excavation 4 was placed 60 m northeast of Excavation 3 at the highest point in Midden 4. It extended westward through four sections designated G1 to G4. Its surface sloped slightly upwards. Refuse was encountered to a depth of 125 cm in Section G1, 103 cm in Section G2 and to 100 cm in Sections G3 and G4 (Figure 5, D). The soil was again dark brown and flecked with bits of ash and charcoal; the subsoil was yellowish brown. Field stones were more frequent than in Excavation 3 and many were fire cracked. Pieces of coral, fossil wood and flint were scattered throughout. Shells and animal bones had the same range and frequency as in Excavation 3. Crab remains were equally rare.

The artifacts total 4,680, of which 4,363 are ceramic, 292 lithic, 22 shell and three bone.

Excavation 5. The work in the two largest middens, which extend along the downhill edge of the site, remains to be considered. Midden 5 occupies the entire northeast quadrant of the ring, closest to the creek (Figure 3). It is 64 m long. Only a quarter of it is on the plateau; the rest spills halfway down the slope leading to the creek. The occupants of this part of the site appear to have lived on the plateau and to have thrown their refuse onto and over its edge.

Excavation 5 was laid out at the highest point in the midden, 55 m east of Excavation 4 (Figure 3). It consisted of four 2 sq m sections extending southwest parallel to the short axis of the midden. These were designated I1 to I4. The surfaces sloped slightly upwards through Sections I1 and I2 on the hillside and then slightly downwards through Sections I3 and I4 on the plateau. This excavation was the deepest of all, consisting of five 25 cm levels in Sections I1 through I3 and six levels in Section I4. It is the only place where we found the complete sequence of periods of occupation, noted in the next chapter.

The four sections of Level 1 contained the greatest concentration and the broadest range of shells anywhere in the site (Figure 5, E). They were less frequent in the subsequent levels. Level 2 in Section I1 consisted almost entirely of ash; elsewhere, the dark brown earth was only speckled with ash and charcoal. Fire-cracked stones, pieces of coral and fragments of flint were present throughout in large quantities. Animal bones were unusually common in Level 2. There were few crab remains.

The artifacts total 9,634, or which 8,474 are ceramic, 1,106 lithic and 54 shell.

It was during the excavation of Level 2 that Rouse fell ill and had to be hospitalized. His successors did not take as detailed notes, and as a result the information we are able to present about excavation units below Level 2 is sketchy.

Excavation 6. The sixth midden is the largest of all. It fills the entire southeastern part of the ring, beginning on its east-west axis and extending 83 m almost to the north-south axis. Like Midden 5, it follows the contours at the edge of the central plateau, as if the inhabitants had thrown their refuse on and over its edge. Excavation 6 was placed in the northeastern part of this midden, 10 m west of the gully in which the discoverers of the site had made their original find. Both the trench and the gully extended in a westerly direction. The trench was composed of four 2 sq m sections designated P1 through P4.

No record exists of the conditions encountered in this excavation. Evidence of two successive layers of deposition were noted on its walls (Figure 5, F). In the absence of information about the exact relationship of these layers to the artificial 25 cm levels in which the sections were dug, the stratigraphy in Excavation 6 must be considered unreliable (Davis 1988:55).

The number of artifacts totals 5,192, of which 4,442 are ceramic, 672 lithic, 73 shell and one bone.

CHAPTER THREE

THE COLLECTIONS

Periods of Occupation

The Indian Creek site is divisible into three successive periods of occupation, each with its own diagnostic style of pottery. The three periods and the styles that define them have been named after Antiguan sites: the first after Indian Creek, the second after Mill Reef and the third after Mamora Bay (Figure 2).

The following discussion of the periods and their styles is not exhaustive. Pursuant to our chronological objective, we have focused on the ceramic modes and the types of artifacts that define each period. In identifying these modes and types we have worked first with the finds from Excavations 1, 2 and 3, because these have conveniently yielded only material from the Indian Creek, Mill Reef and Mamora Bay periods, respectively. Then we extended the two systems of classification to Excavations 4, 5 and 6, making the necessary adjustments in the two classifications as we proceeded.

In our opinion, it would have been a mistake for us to classify the potsherds themselves into types, as many archaeologists do, because potsherds per se are not parts of cultures. The natives discarded them because they were no longer useful. In effect, we have brought the sherds back into the cultures by analyzing them as culturally significant features and classifying these features to form modes. Ideally, we should also reconstruct vessels from these sherds and classify them into vessel types, but we have not obtained enough reconstructible vessels to do so.

We have counted and tabulated the number of examples of each mode in each section and level of our excavations. These tabulations are too extensive to be presented here and have been deposited in the Yale Peabody Museum's (YPM) files, where they are available to interested scholars and students.

The Indian Creek Period

Excavation 1, Excavation 5, Levels 7–6, and Excavation 6, Levels 6–3, date from the Indian Creek period. The fact that the latter two are at the bottom of their respective excavations confirms the position of this period at the beginning of the sequence of occupations.

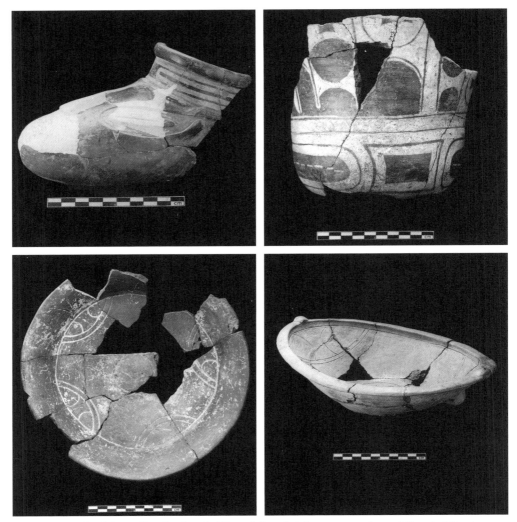

FIGURE 7. Vessels of the Indian Creek style. Upper left and right, wor ware; lower left and right, zic ware. YPM catalog nos.: upper left, 254321; upper right, 254651; lower left, 254634; lower right, 254682.

Pottery Vessels

In his preliminary reports Rouse (1974, 1976, 1978) treated the pottery of the Indian Creek period as a single, homogenous style. It has since been found to be divisible into two wares, each named after a distinctive mode of decoration: white-on-red ware, abbreviated to "wor"; and zoned incised crosshatched ware, abbreviated to "zic." Wor ware dominates; zic ware comprises less than 10% of the sherds recovered from the component. Both wares occurred together in all of the excavation units.

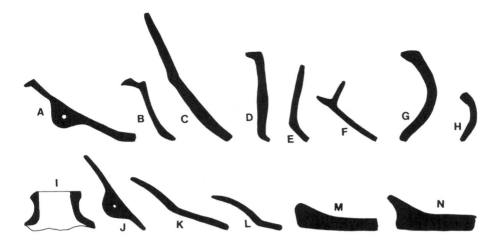

FIGURE 8. Rim profiles, Indian Creek period. A–F, wor ware bowls; G, H, wor ware jars; I, wor ware bottle; J–L, zic ware bowls; M, N, griddles.

WOR WARE

Material. The sherds of this ware are relatively fine and thin. Their thickness, which varies little from one part of the pot to another, falls mostly between 5 and 6 mm. Fractures are firm and regular. The temper consists of fine particles of grit. Surfaces are smooth and relatively hard, but not polished. They show no traces of the coiling process, and there is little evidence of breakage along the coils. The better sherds ring when struck together.

Shape. The range of shapes is greater than in the subsequent components, including bowls (Figure 8, A–F), jars (Figure 8, G, H; Figure 7, upper right) and bottles (Figure 8, I). Most of the bowls had outsloping sides; upcurving sides rank second and incurving sides a distant third (Figure 7). There is also a boot-shaped vessel (Figure 7, upper left).

Bases were either round, flat or annular (Figure 9, E, F, G); and bodies, hemispherical. Relatively few of the bodies terminated directly in rims; instead, shoulders were added to form bowls, or shoulders and necks to form either jars or bottles. The keels separating the bodies and shoulders were relatively unobtrusive. Outsloping-sided, keeled bowls often had concave shoulders, which gave the whole vessel an S-shaped profile and the appearance of an inverted bell.

The shoulders of bowls terminated either in rims or in concave flanges, projecting outwards from the body of the vessel. Alternatively, a rectangular ridge might be attached to either the inside or the outside of the rim (Figure 9, M). Bowl rims were round, flat or triangular in cross section; some had been twisted or perforated (Figure 9, L, R). Flange and jar rims tended to be round.

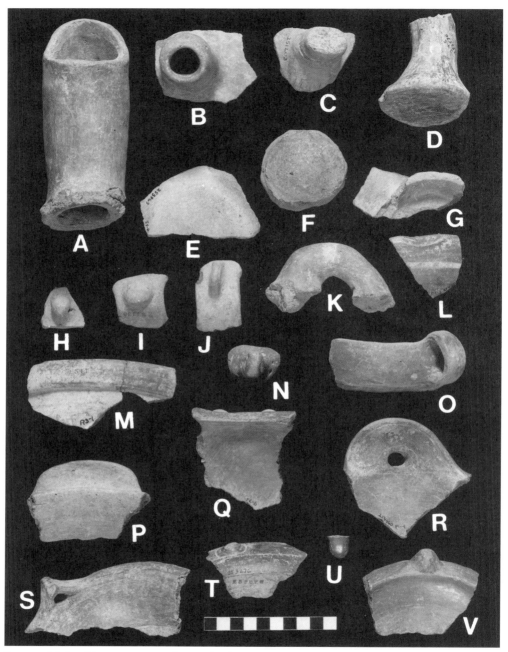

FIGURE 9. Modes of shape, wor ware, Indian Creek style. A, B, spouts; C, D, feet; E, F, flat bases; G, annular base; H, lump pierced for suspension; I–K, O handles; L, twisted rim; M, rectangular ridge on a rim; N, bird's head lug; P, semicircular lug beneath the rim; Q, raised side of a turtle bowl; R, semicircular, perforated lug; S, animal-head lug on a strap-shaped projection; T, incised and punctated lump on a flange; U, small prong-shaped lug; V, conical lug. YPM catalog nos.: A, 254640; B, 254782; C, 251203; D, 253570; E, 253969; F, 254604; G, 251868; H, 251291; I, 251130; J, 251334; K, 254537; L, 254283; M, 251128; N, 251142; O, 254482; P, 251368; Q, 254816; R, 254460; S, 254818; T, 253278; U, 254379; V, 251408.

Additions to the exterior walls of the vessels included legs of indeterminate shape (Figure 9, C, D), strap or, less commonly, rod handles (Figure 9, J, K, O), lumps pierced for suspension (Figure 9, H) and spouts (Figure 9, A, B). Rectangular or semi-circular tabs, some of them perforated, were attached to rims or, less commonly, to keels (Figure 9, P, R). Alternatively, rims were adorned with relatively small, zoomorphic head lugs (Figure 9, N, S) and faced either inwards or outwards. Round or prismatic in shape, many of them have deeply hollow backs. Also present are conical lugs (Figure 9, U, V) and fragments of turtle-shaped bowls with a head in the front, a pair of raised sides ending in flippers, and a tail in the rear (Figure 9, Q).

Decoration. A dark red slip dominates, usually limited to the outside or the inside of the vessel, or to a single element of shape, such as a base, shoulder or rim (Figure 10, A, E). Overall, red slip increases markedly in frequency from the bottom to the top of Excavation 1, foreshadowing the trend during the subsequent Mill Reef period.

White-painted designs are limited to the outside of the vessel. They have been placed in red-painted zones or else alongside them in the form of a thin white line bordering the zone (Figure 10, B–D, F). Many of the motifs in the zones are negative (Figure 10, D, H). Hourglasses and spirals are common motifs (Figure 13; Figure 10, I, J). Orange or black paint was sometimes added, creating polychrome designs (Figure 10, G, O, S–U). Incision is more important than in most Saladoid styles. Its grooves are fine and relatively shallow (Figure 11, A, G) and occur on either the inside or the outside of the vessel. They depict simple geometric designs, such as parallel lines just below the rim, spirals, or an ovoid figure consisting of an oval line enclosing a horizontal line (Figure 10, M, U). A punctation was occasionally added at each end of the horizontal line or adjacent to it (Figure 11, D). There are several examples of excision. The incised grooves were sometimes filled with white paint and occur on vessel walls or on flanges, handles or lugs (Figure 10, L, M, P–R). The trait was widespread through the Lesser Antilles and the eastern part of the Greater Antilles in late Saladoid time. On Antigua, it also persists from the Indian Creek period into the beginning of the Mill Reef period.

Finally, the potters of the Indian Creek period employed the technique of modeling, often in combination with incision and/or punctation, to depict the features of head lugs (Figure 11, C, E, F, H, N, P, R, S) and to decorate flanges (Figure 10, T, U) or the outside walls of vessels (Figure 11, M, Q). The motifs on the flanges and walls consist of dimpled lumps of clay encircled by single lines, spirals, and limbs extending downwards from the rim.

This combination of modeling, incision and/or punctation is widespread among the Saladoid inhabitants of the Windward Islands. Some designs may have originated there; others may be the result of influence from the Barrancoid peoples, who were expanding at the time from the Orinoco Valley to northern Guiana, the eastern Venezuelan coast and the island of Trinidad. There is good evidence that the Barrancoid intruders opened up trade with the Saladoid peoples of the Lesser Antilles as far north as Antigua (Morse and Rouse, 1999). Barrancoid trade sherds were en-

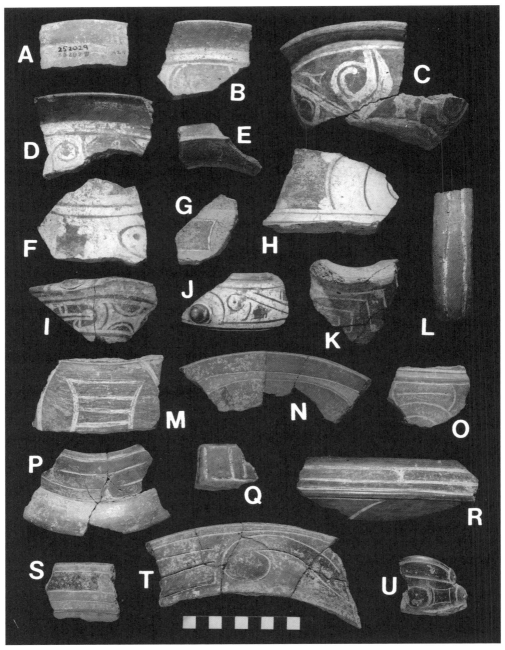

FIGURE 10. Modes of decoration, wor ware, Indian Creek style. A, E, red paint on a plain surface; B, D, F, H–J, white-on-red painting; C, K, R, white-on-red on plain; G, white-on-red on orange; L, P, Q, red slip with white in incised grooves; M, R, white in incised grooves; N, red bordered by incision; O, orange with white-on-red; S–U, black on red. All except T are on outer surfaces. YPM catalog nos.: A, 252029; B, 251338; C, 253795; D, 254809; E, 251431; F, 254053; G, 254611; H, 254053; I, 254819; J, 253687; K, 254414; L, 254814; M, 254672; N, 252030; O, 253273; P, 254748; Q, 254780; R, 254469; S, 251353; T, 254289; U, 254624.

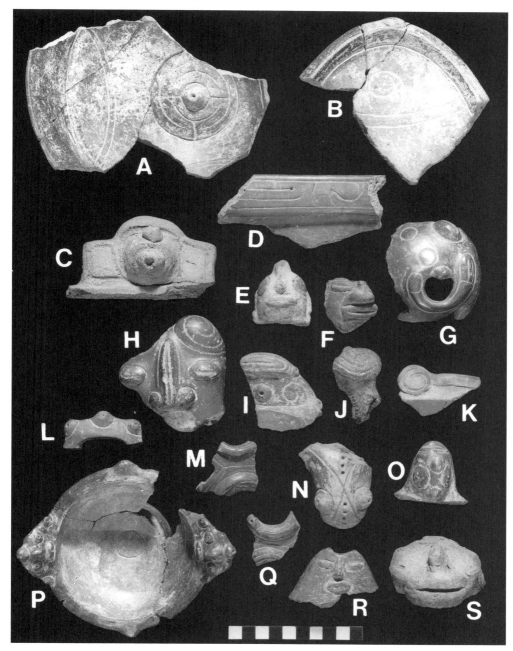

FIGURE 11. Modes of decoration (continued), wor ware, Indian Creek style. A,B, incision on interior walls; C, modeled-incised head on a rectangular tab; D, incised design on the interior beneath a flange; E, F, H, N–P, R, S, modeled head lugs; G, I–K, M, Q, modeling-incision on exterior walls; L, modeling-incision on a rectangular tab. YPM catalog nos.: A, 254664; B, 254526; C, 254627; D, 254599; E, 254628; F, 251191; G, 254786; H, 253686; I, 254574; J, 254038; K, 251201; L, 254213; M, 254680; N, 254626; O, 254629; P, 254795; Q, 254652; R, 253685; S, 253868.

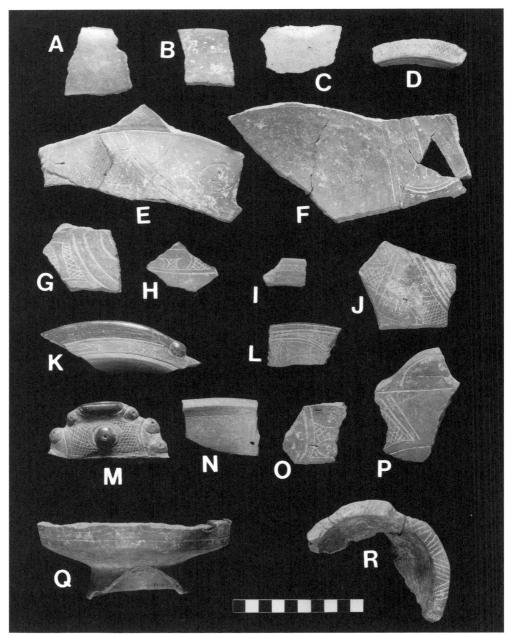

FIGURE 12. Modes of shape and decoration, zic ware, Indian Creek style. A, B, open bowls; C, flat base; D, I, incised crosshatching on a flange; B, G, H, J, incised crosshatching on vessel interiors; F, L, O, incision and red paint on vessel interiors; K, incision and red paint on a flange; M, incision and red paint on a lug; N, incision on vessel interior; P, incision and red paint on vessel interior and on a flange: Q, annular-base bowl with incision on the interior; R, incision on vessel rim. YPM catalog nos.: A, 254020; B, 251015; C, 254703; D, 251394; E, 254627; F, 254514; G, 253964; H, 254700; I, 254698; J, 254709; K, 254677; L, 254700; M, 254625; N, 251360; O, 254566; P, 254556; Q, 254784; R, 254536.

FIGURE 13. White-on-red painted design, Indian Creek period.

countered in the top level of Excavation 1 and in the Indian Creek period levels of Excavations 5 and 6, surviving into the early Mill Reef period components of those excavations (Figure 17, N, O). Similar specimens have been found on the island of Nevis just west of Antigua (Samuel Wilson, personal communication 1997). We know of no finds farther north in the Leeward Islands.

ZIC WARE

Originally, we were able to identify as zic ware only sherds that were decorated with zoned incised crosshatching. As we became more familiar with the collection, we learned also to use criteria of material, shape and other aspects of decoration, as follows.

Material. Zic ware sherds are as fine as the best of the wor ware and sometimes as thin as 4.5 mm. They have a lighter, tan color and, because they are softer, do not ring when struck together. The sherds appear to be sparsely tempered with fine grit or sand. Surfaces are smooth but slightly uneven, and fractures are firm, granular and relatively straight.

Shape. Bowls are the only vessel type. They were basically hemispherical, with the rare exception of an oval or boat shape (Figure 7, lower left, lower right). Bottoms are round, flat or annular (Figure 12, C, Q). Slight keels, narrow shoulders and an occasional flange were often built into them (Figure 16, K, L). More open and shallower than wor ware bowls, they had similar handles and lugs (Figure 16, J).

Decoration. Given the openness and shallowness of the zic ware bowls, the potters decorated them mostly on the inside, often just beneath the rim (Figure 12, L), on the rim top (Figure 12, R) or on flanges (Figure 12, D, I, K). Like the wor ware potters,

FIGURE 14. Griddles, cylinders, other types of clay artifacts, and types of stone and shell artifacts, Indian Creek period. A, shell celt; B, shell spoon; C, possible shell pendant; D, E, undrilled shell beads; F, shell pendant; G, shell disk, presumably inlaid in wood to portray an eye of an idol; H, shell three-pointer; I, shell sliver ground to a point at one end; J–L, shell pendants; M, sherd of an incense burner, decorated with a white-painted design; N, P, Q, griddle sherds; O, part of an incense burner, showing the hole in the top; R, bit of a stone celt; S, flint chip with traces of use; T, butt of a stone celt reused as a hammer; U, pitted hammerstone; V, top of an incense burner decorated with a band of red paint just beneath the rim. YPM catalog nos.: A, 251415; B, 252033; C, 253838; D, 254824; E, 252029; F, 252032; G, 254495; H, 253838; I, 252035; J, 252027; K, 254492; L, 253838; M, 253970; N, 251365; O, 254456; P, 251365; Q, 251306; R, 254016; S, 251060; T, 253954; U, 251413; V, 244714.

they produced zoned as well as linear designs and outlined the zones with heavy incised lines, but filled the zones with incised crosshatching rather than with paint. The zones portray similar parallel line, hourglass and spiral motifs (Figure 12, G, H, L, O). The ovoid linear motif so typical of wor ware is absent.

While zic ware is normally without paint, an appreciable number of our finds bear a red slip like that on wor ware (Figure 12, F, K, L, O, P). Red-painted zones are often placed alongside zic zones, as if to contrast the two modes of decoration (Figure 12, L, K, M). Petersen (personal communication), Wilson (personal communication) and Versteeg and Schinkel (1992) have found similar breakdowns between the two wares at the Trants site on Montserrat, the Hickman site on Nevis and the Golden Rock site on St. Eustatius, respectively. The Antigua breakdowns are limited to the Indian Creek period but those on the other three islands may have survived later (unpublished data from a paper presented at the Seventeenth International Congress for Caribbean Archaeology, July 25–29, 1997, Nassau, Bahamas).

SHARED TRAITS

The better made sherds of both wares are thin, hard, smooth surfaced and finely grit or sand tempered. They also share distinctive features of shape: hemispherical bowls, keels and flanges; the zoning of designs; filling of the zones (whether by painting or crosshatching); D-shaped, peg-topped strap handles; circular and button lugs; and zoomorphic head lugs.

Other Kinds of Clay Artifacts

Fragments of griddles for baking cassava bread and of cylinders that may have served as incense burners were found throughout the Indian Creek period deposits. The griddle sherds come from flat, heavy disks ranging from 20 to more than 40 cm in diameter and from 1 to 2 cm in thickness. The tops of these disks were smooth, their bottoms rough, and a few were mat impressed. They had thickened, slightly raised rims, most of which are triangular in cross section (Figure 8, M, N; Figure 14, N, P, Q). The exceptions are flat or round. There is no decoration.

The cylinders varied from 10 to over 20 cm in diameter. They had relatively thick walls, ranging from slightly less than 1 to almost 2 cm in thickness and were open at one end and closed at the other. The open end was often ridged on the outside in order to strengthen it. Traces of wear indicate that this end was placed on the ground. The closed end had a hole for the exit of smoke or incense (Figure 14, O, V). From the presence of T-shaped sherds it may be inferred that the walls of some cylinders projected above their closed ends. A few fragments are decorated with red-painted, white-on-red painted, and incised designs like those on the pottery vessels (Figure 14, M, V).

STONE ARTIFACTS

The Indian Creek period deposits yielded only parts of stone celts (Figure 14, R), several of them reused as hammers (Figure 14, T); hammerstones, several of them pitted

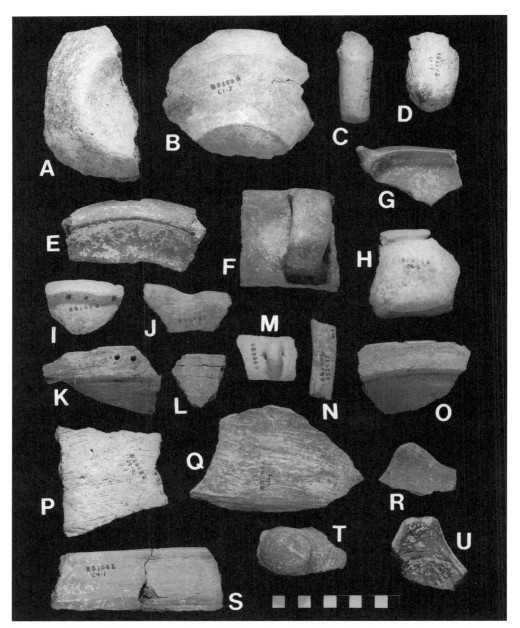

FIGURE 15. Modes of shape and surface finish, Mill Reef style. A, dimpled base; B, flat base; C, D, cylindrical legs; E, flange; F, N, D-shaped strap handles; G, boat-shaped bowl decorated with a conical lug and with red paint extending part way down from the lug and rim onto the interior wall of the vessel; H, keel of a bowl decorated with a turtle flipper; I, perforated keel of a bowl; J, K, twisted rims; L, corrugated rim sherd; M, lump on the outside of a vessel, pierced for suspension; O, triangular rim with red paint that extends onto the inner wall; P, scratched sherd; Q, scratched and red-painted sherd; R,U, tabular lugs; S, scored sherd; T, cylindrical lug. YPM catalog nos.: A, 251601; B, 251698; C, 251544; D, 251701; E, 251807; F, 254416; G, 251701; H, 251673; I, 251674; J, 251752; K, 253137; L, 251541; M, 252557; N, 252592; O, 251725; P, 251671; Q, 251834; R, 251752; S, 251541; T, 251602; U, 251493.

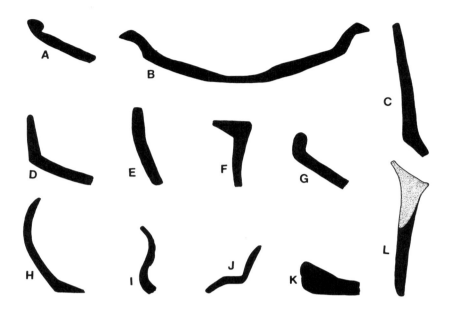

FIGURE 16. Rim profiles, Mill Reef period. A–I, bowls; J, jar; K, plain griddle; L, legged griddle.

(Figure 14, U); two undrilled stone beads (Figure 14, D, E); and a small, crudely finished three-pointer, also known as a *zemi* (Figure 14, H). A few of the flint chips scattered through the deposit show traces of having been used as scraping or cutting tools (Figure 14, S). They are usually roundish or triangular in shape, vary in size from 4 to 7 cm, and seem to have had only a single cutting edge. There are no bone artifacts.

SHELL ARTIFACTS

Shell was the preferred material for making celts (Figure 14, A). Each was produced by grinding a bevel on one end of the lip of a conch shell (*Strombus gigas*). They vary in length from 10 to almost 20 cm. This type is characteristic of the previous Archaic Age inhabitants of the Lesser Antilles, who presumably transmitted it to the Saladoid invaders. Olive shells were cut in the form of spoons (Figure 14, B). A sliver of conch shell has been ground to a point at one end (Figure 14, I).

Ornaments lacked decoration. Olive and cowrie shells were strung as beads, and both olive and mother of pearl shells were perforated for use as pendants (Figure 14, J, K). Other pendants were made of conch shell (Figure 14, F, L).

Several plain three-pointers of shell were found in Indian Creek component. They have been made from the prongs of *Strombus gigas* shells by breaking off, cutting and/or grinding their bases so as to enable them to stand upright (Figure 14, H). No working of any kind is visible on their sides or points. One small disk resembles those inlayed in the heads of protohistoric wooden idols to portray their eyes (Figure 14, G).

FIGURE 17. Modes of decoration, Mill Reef style. A, B, F, linear white-on-red painted designs; C, D, zoned white-on-red painted designs; E, white on plain design; G, white-on-red design on a plain surface; H, J, white-on-red and black design; I, white-on-black and orange design; K, incised and red-painted design; L, incised design beneath a row of perforations; M, white-on-red painted design combined with incision; N, O, presumed Barrancoid trade sherds; P, mask modeled on a vessel wall; Q, R, crudely modeled zoomorphic lugs; S, modeled-incised tabular lug. YPM catalog nos.: A, 251603; B, 251505; C, 251963; D, 254046; E, 253316; F, 251791; G, 251819; H, 254049; I, 253232; J, 254049; K, 254096; L, 251739; M, 251617; N, 253271; O, 253527; P, 254312; Q, 251470; R, 251668; S, 251744.

Mill Reef Period

This period was encountered throughout Excavation 2 and in Levels 5 and 4 of Excavation 4, Levels 5 and 4 of Excavation 5, and Levels 2 and 1 of Excavation 6. The Excavation 5 deposits overlie Indian Creek period deposits and underlie Mamora Bay period deposits, providing a complete record of the sequence of periods.

Pottery Vessels
Wor is the only ware present in the Mill Reef deposits. Zic ware disappeared at the end of the Indian Creek period.

Material. The quality of the sherds deteriorates. They tend to be thicker and coarser; none is less than 6 mm thick. There is also greater variation; the flat base of one sherd measures 20 mm in thickness and the wall immediately above it only 9 mm. Fractures are less regular and more crumbly. Larger particles of grit were used as tempering material. The sherds are poorly finished. Coils are not always completely fused. Many of the surfaces are soft and cream-colored, resembling in these respects the pottery of the contemporaneous Cuevas style in Puerto Rico. The Mill Reef pottery is otherwise quite different, however.

Shape. The number of kinds of vessels is reduced to bowls and an occasional jar (Figure 16, J). Boat-shaped bowls are still popular (Figure 15, B) and outsloping sides continue to predominate (Figure 16, A–I). Their features tend to be more angular than before, as in the contemporaneous Ostionoid pottery of the Greater Antilles.

Dimpled bases now become an alternative to flat bases (Figure 15, A, B). There are also a few cylindrical legs but no longer any annular bases (Figure 15, C, D). Keels retain their popularity (Figure 15, H, I, K, Q). The shoulders above them tend to be narrower than in Saladoid pottery, perhaps because it was no longer the practice to decorate them with such elaborate designs (Figure 15, B). Many of the shoulders of outsloping-sided bowls are still concavo-convex, giving their vessels the appearance of inverted bells (Figure 16, B). Rim flanges continue as before (Figure 15, E; Figure 16, F).

The twisting of rims persists (Figure 15, J, K), as do semicircular and rectangular tabs (Figure 15, R, U), conical and cylindrical lugs (Figure 15, G, T), lumps of clay perforated for suspension (Figure 15, M) and strap handles (Figure 15, F, N). The strap handles no longer have pegs on top. Head lugs have also disappeared. One sherd has a row of perforations through a ridge on the keel, and another, through the wall just beneath the rim.

Decoration. A new dimension is introduced into the decoration: surface finish. This may be considered diagnostic not only of the Mill Reef style but also of the subsequent Mamora Bay and Freeman's Bay styles, that is, of the Mamoran Troumassoid subseries of styles that succeeded the Cedrosan Saladoid subseries in the Leeward Islands.

Whereas the Saladoid potters had valued smooth surfaces, the Mamoran

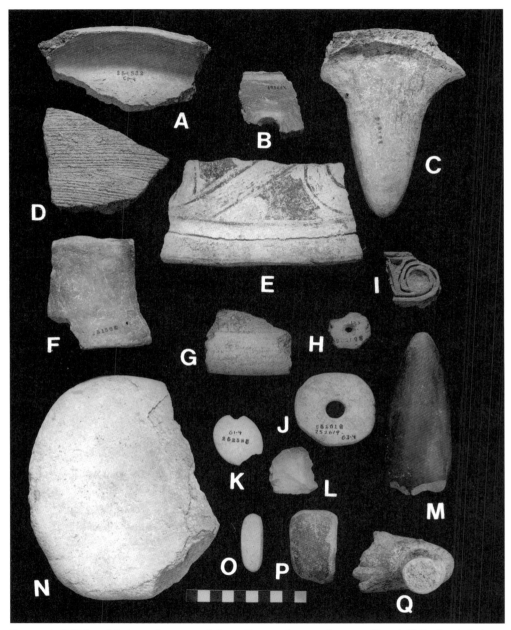

FIGURE 18. Griddles, clyinders, other types of clay artifacts, and types of stone artifacts, Mill Reef period. A, top view of a griddle rim sherd; B, red-painted sherd from the top of a cylinder, showing the central opening; C, griddle leg; D, scratched bottom of a griddle; E, basal part of a cylinder, painted white-on-red; F, basal part of a cylinder, undecorated; G, rectangular base of a cylinder; H, red-painted and drilled clay disk; I, clay stamp; J, plain, drilled clay disk; K, stone net-sinker; L, flint chip with traces of use; M, stone celt; N, stone metate; O, rectangularly ground piece of conch shell; P, worn out stone celt used as a hammer; Q, foot of a vessel or a clay idol, painted white-on-red. YPM catalog nos.: A, 251832; B, 253569; C, 251676; D, 251779; E, 253546; F, 251563; G, 251911; H, 251500; I, 251558; J, 252619; K, 252585; L, 251770; M, 254088; N, 251746; O, 251873: P, 254089; Q, 252977.

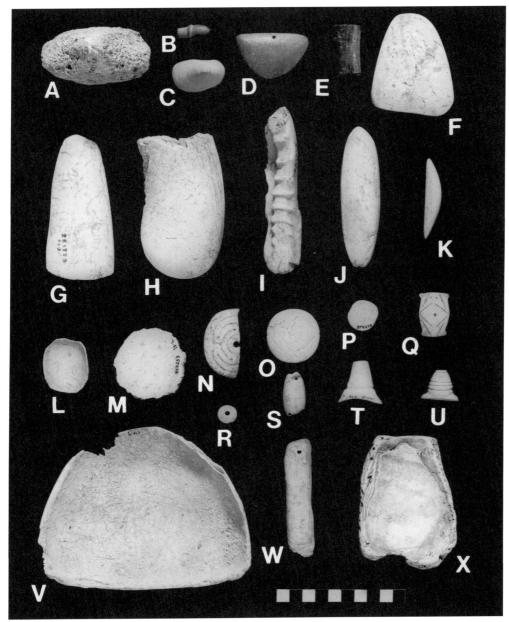

FIGURE 19. Types of stone artifacts (continued), and bone and shell artifacts, Mill Reef period. A, three-pointer of coral; B, penis-shaped object of stone; C, three-pointer of stone; D, perforated greenstone pendant; E, cut, animal bone bead; F, tortoise shell spatula; G, H, shell celts; I, shell chisel; J, celt-shaped piece of shell, grooved on the bit; K, bi-pointed artifact of shell; L, shell spoon; M, P, plain shell disks; N, O, incised shell disks; Q, frog pendant of shell; R, shell spoon; S, oliva shell pendant; T, U, shell three-pointers, both incised; V, X, shell vessels; W, razor shell pendant. YPM catalog nos.: A, 251639; B, 151746; C, 253408; D, 251873; E, 252558; F, 252672; G, 251772; H, 253252; I, 251875; J, 251747; K, 254244; L, 254419; M, 253253; N, 251830; O, 251747; P, 254272; Q, 252653; R, S, 252614; T, 253345; U, 252653; V, 251830; W, 252674; X, 524083.

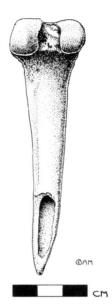

©AM

CM

FIGURE 20. Dog bone pick, Mill Reef period.

potters preferred to texture theirs, either by scratching, scoring or corrugating them, or by painting them in streaks. The scratching was done by drawing a fine-toothed comb along the surface of the wet clay to produce parallel line patterns (Figure 15, P, Q). A blunt tool was used to score the surfaces (Figure 15, S). Corrugation was produced by incompletely fusing the coils used to build up the walls of vessels (Figure 15, L). Scratching was by far the most popular of these techniques; corrugation was rare.

Red slip continued to be a prominent feature of the surface finish. It could still be limited to a single feature of the vessel, such as the inside or outside of a base, shoulder or rim, but was more often used overall (Figure 15, O). It occurs not only on plain surfaces but also on scratched, scored or incised surfaces (Figure 15, Q). Lighter in color and thinner than the Saladoid slip, it might better be called a wash since it was brushed on lightly in the form of streaks. This contributed to the textured appearance, especially when the wash was applied to cream-colored surfaces.

White-painted designs also persisted, contrary to the situation in the contemporaneous Ostionoid series of the Greater Antilles, and tended to be less carefully executed than before. Many were still zoned (Figure 17, C–E, G, H). The Saladoid practice of bordering white-painted zones with thin, curvilinear white lines also continued to be popular. White-and-red painted zones were sometimes juxtaposed on a plain background (Figure 17, G) and were occasionally accompanied by black-painted zones (Figure 17, H, J). Orange paint was less common (Figure 17, I). We have noticed no changes in either the form or the frequency of the zoned designs from the beginning to the end of the Mill Reef period.

New to the period were simple rectilinear designs, consisting mostly of isolated groups of parallel white lines, broadly and crudely painted on either a red or a plain background (Figure 17, A, B, F). This kind of white-on-red painting persisted into the subsequent Mamora Bay period. In effect, the Mill Reef potters combined their Saladoid predecessors' tradition of zoned painting with a new linear tradition, and passed on both traditions to their Mamora Bay successors.

Incision now became a more important part of the decoration. In Excavation 2, which yielded only pottery of the Mill Reef style, the frequency of this technique increases from 3.1% of the decoration in Level 5 to 17.3% in Level 1; 56% of the designs are rectilinear and 33% curvilinear, a percentage that does not change from the bottom to the top of the excavation. There is one example of excision.

The incised lines continue to be relatively shallow and fine-lined. They are still used either to outline painted zones or to delineate designs, which range from horizontal parallel lines to complex curvilinear figures, among them the ovoid motif (Figure 17, L, M). At the beginning of the Mill Reef period white paint continues to be placed in the grooves of red-slipped sherds in order to accentuate them. The same effect was obtained later in the period by incising through red slip into a cream-colored paste (Figure 17, K).

To Saladoid-type incision is now added another kind, diagnostic of both the Mill Reef and the Mamora Bay styles and hence of all local units within the Mamoran Troumassoid subseries. Its grooves are broader and deeper and its designs larger, simpler and bolder. The designs consist typically of horizontal parallel lines placed just beneath the rim on either the inside or the outside of the vessel. There are also a few curvilinear motifs, the form and location of which cannot be determined because they extend too far beyond the limits of individual sherds.

Lugs have become rare. They include flat, rectangular or semicircular tabs, a few of which are still incised and punctated with geometric designs (Figure 17, S). New to this period are elongated vertical ridges crudely modeled into zoomorphic heads (Figure 17, Q, R). A human face is crudely modeled on a vessel wall (Figure 17, P).

Broad, shallow incision, horizontal parallel lines beneath the rim, and the human face design may be the influence from the peoples of the Barrancoid series, who expanded during Mill Reef time from their homeland in the lower Orinoco Valley to the Guiana coast and the islands of Trinidad and Tobago. There they developed a trading system that extended northwards through the Windward Islands to Antigua and Nevis at the entry into the Leewards (Rouse 1992:85; Samuel Wilson, personal communication, 1997). Several typically Barrancoid series sherds we encountered in the Mill Reef component may have been products of this trading system (Figure 17, N, O).

Other Kinds of Clay Artifacts
Griddles continued to be used to bake cassava bread (Figure 18, A). To the ubiquitous disk-shaped griddles of the previous period (Figure 16, K), which were presumably supported over the fire by large stones, were now added a new, tripod type in which flat, triangular legs took the place of stone supports (Figure 16, L; Figure 18, C). The roughness of the lower surfaces of both kinds of griddles was sometimes accentuated

by scratching or by mat impression (Figure 18, D). The bottom of one griddle shows evidence of coiling. Rims are still triangular or occasionally round; none is flat (Figure 16, K, L).

Clay cylinders or incense burners were still produced (Figure 18, B, F). They have the same elements of shape as before, including rectangular ridges at their bases (Figure 18, G), but some of the rough lower surfaces are now scratched (Figure 18, D) or, more rarely, corrugated. Also new to the Mill Reef period are red, white and\or black designs painted in zones on the outsides of cylinders (Figure 18, E). They are occasionally bordered by incised lines.

Clay stamps make their first appearance with three examples of irregular or pronged sherds deeply incised on one side (Figure 18, I). We also obtained nine disks of clay, five of them drilled as if for use as spindle whorls (Figure 18, H, J). Another is too large to have served that purpose; it may have been the partially finished, flat base of a vessel. There are also two feet from large clay vessels or figurines (Figure 18, Q).

STONE ARTIFACTS

The Mill Reef period artisans did little stonework. We recovered only two celts of that material; one shows traces of use as a hammer after its bit had been worn away (Figure 18, M, P). Two irregularly shaped pebbles have grinding facets and five show traces of hammering. Several notched stones may have been used as net-sinkers (Figure 18, K). There are three metates, one rectangular and the other two irregularly shaped (Figure 18, N). A few flint chips show traces of use (Figure 18, L).

One small, finely made semicircular pendant is drilled for suspension just beneath its top edge (Figure 19, D). A tinier specimen has been ground into the form of a penis (Figure 19, B). Two small, plain three-pointers are made of coral limestone (Figure 19, A, C).

BONE ARTIFACTS

Two long bones of dogs have been cut and ground on one end to form pick-like tools, presumably for use in processing soft materials (Figure 20). One piece of unidentified long bone has been worked into the form of a bead (Figure 19, E). A sliver of manatee bone bears a nicely carved zoomorphic head design (Figure 21).

SHELL ARTIFACTS

Shell continued to be the preferred material for making both tools and ornaments. Excavation 2 yielded 11 celts and a celt blank (Figure 19, G, H), a chisel (Figure 19, I), a hammer made from the lip of a conch shell (*Strombus gigas*) battered on one end, and a ground, bi-pointed object, possibly made to be hafted in a spear or arrow (Figure 19, K). We also obtained a spoon (Figure 19, L) and two vessels each made from half of the body of a conch shell (Figure 19, V, X). Oliva and razor-shaped shells have been perforated for use as pendants (Figure 19, S, W) and a piece of conch shell is carved in the form of a frog (Figure 19, Q).

Three rectangular and five discoidal pieces of conch shell were recovered. The

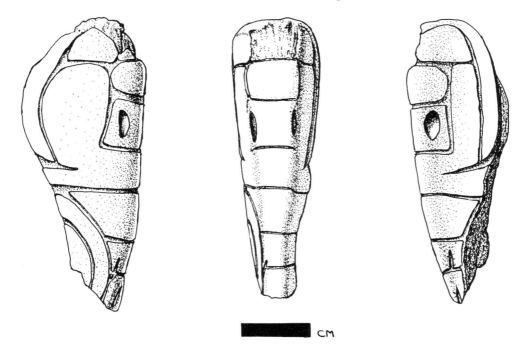

FIGURE 21. Carved bone figure, Mill Reef period.

three rectangular pieces and two of the disks (Figure 19, M, P) are plain. One plain disk is small enough to have been inlaid into wood to form the eye of an idol (Figure 19, P). Three of the disks are geometrically incised (Figure 19, N, O); one of them is also punctated (Figure 19, N). A piece of turtle shell cut in the form of a spatula (Figure 19, F) and two small, incised three-pointers (Figure 19, T, U) may have been used in the worship of zemis.

Mamora Bay Period

Refuse of this period was encountered throughout Midden 3, in Levels 3–1 at the top of Excavation 4, and in Levels 3–1 at the top of Excavation 5. Relatively few traits inherited from the Cedrosan Saladoid subseries survive. Hence, the culture is typically Mamoran Troumassoid, as the name of the period implies.

Pottery Vessels

Material. The quality of the sherds continues to be poor. They are still coarse and vary in thickness from one part of the vessel to another. The tempering consist of large particles of grit. As before, the sherds are poorly finished. The soft, cream-colored paste disappears; all the sherds are now hard and gritty and tend to be thicker.

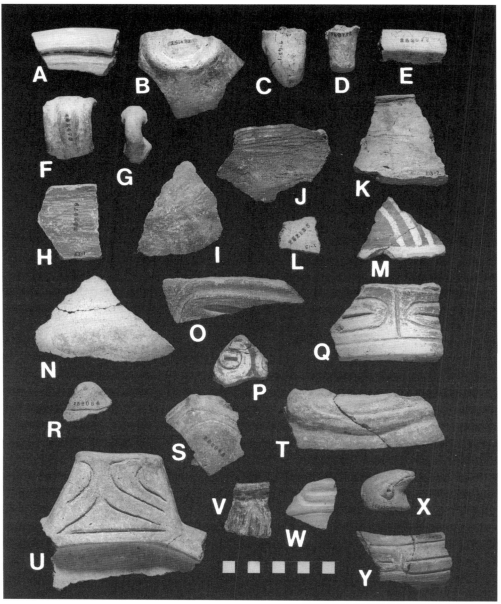

FIGURE 22. Modes of shape and decoration, Mamora Bay style. A, folded rim; B, dimpled base; C, D, cylindrical legs; E, flanged rim; F, strap handle; G, rod handle; H, overall red paint; I, red and black paint; J, scratched sherd; K, scored sherd; L, white slip; M, N, linear white-on-red painting; O,Q,T, red paint on incision; P, white-on-red zoned painting; R, red-painted semicircular tab; S, red-painted, modeled-incised design; U, incision on a rectangular tab; V, crude modeling on vessel wall; W, ovoid incision on vessel wall; X, modeled bird's head lug; Y, incised ovoid design. YPM catalog nos.: A, 252350; B, 252183; C, 252319; D, 252895; E, 252077; F, 252475; G, 252822; H, 252079; I, 252114; J, 252113; K, 252182; L, 252135; M, 252096; O, 252060; P, 252771; Q, 252324; R, 252060; P, 252771; Q, 252324; R, 252084; S, 252042; T, 252756; U, 253132; V, 252978; W, 252200; X, 252339; Y, 252364.

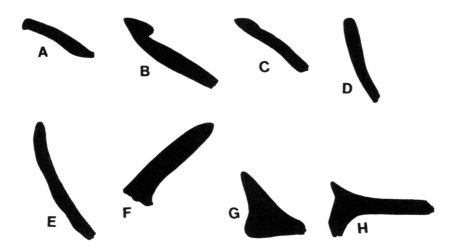

FIGURE 23. Rim profiles, Mamora Bay period. A–F, bowls; G, simple griddle; H, legged griddle.

Shape. Bowls continue to predominate over jars and to have mostly outsloping sides (Figure 23, A–F). Bases, keels, shoulders and flanges are unchanged (Figure 22, B–E). Some rims are now loosely folded inwards (Figure 22, A; Figure 23, B). All of the shape modifications inherited from the Saladoid series have disappeared except for plain strap or rod handles and semicircular or rectangular tabs (Figure 22, F, G, R, U). Bird's head lugs persist from the subsequent Mill Reef period (Figure 22, X).

Decoration. Scratching, scoring, and red slip remain common (Figure 22, J, K, H) and corrugation becomes more popular. There are a considerable number of examples of white slip (Figure 22, L) and of white designs on a red slip or on a plain background; these designs are mostly linear (Figure 22, M). There are only a few examples of Saladoid zoning (Figure 22, P). Some black- and red-painted zones are juxtaposed (Figure 22, I).

Incised lines are now broad and deep, so much so that the potters were able to sloppily paint them red instead of filling them with paint (Figure 22, O, Q, S, T). Designs are both curvilinear and rectilinear. Incised ovoid designs recall earlier forms but are more poorly executed (Figure 22, W, Y). One sherd bears a pair of molded ridges, possibly representing legs (Figure 22, V).

Other Kinds of Clay Artifacts
Both plain and legged griddles continued to be made (Figure 23, G, H; Figure 24, A, B). Their rough bottoms are often scratched; rims are triangular in cross section or in one case round.

The sherds from cylinders are difficult to distinguish from thick potsherds (Figure 24, C). They have either flat, round or triangular rims. Some are still decorated,

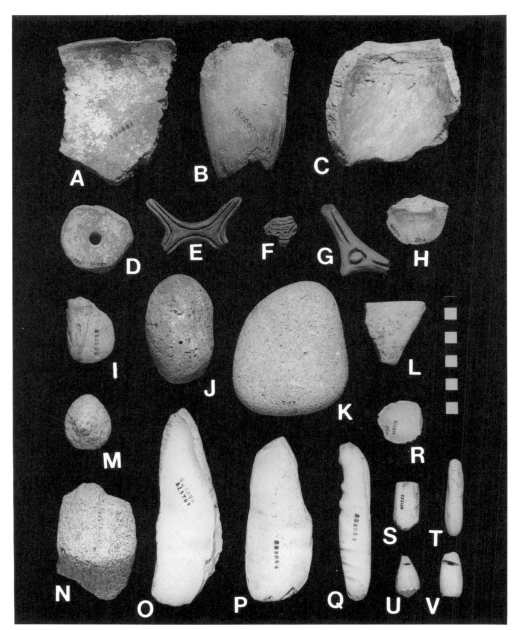

FIGURE 24. Griddles, cylinders, other types of clay artifacts, and types of stone and shell artifacts, Mamora Bay period. A, griddle rim sherd; B, griddle leg sherd; C, rim sherd from a cylinder; D, drilled, red-painted clay disk; E–G, clay stamps; H, flint flake showing signs of use; I, bit of stone celt; J, K, hammerstones; L, grinding stone; M, N, three-pointers made from coral limestone; O, P, shell celts; Q, shell chisel; R, shell disk; S, rectangular shell artifact; T, cylindrical shell object; U,V, oliva shell pendants. YPM catalog nos.: A, 252057; B, 252080; C, 252271; D, 252989; E, 252184; F, 251300; G, 252275; H, 252914; I, 252198; J, 252179; K, 252194; L, 252996; M, 252194; N, 252760; O, 252179; P, Q, 252054; R, 252817; U, 252179; V, 252134.

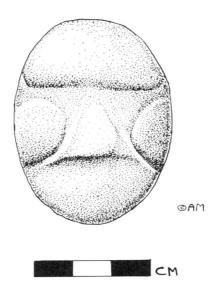

FIGURE 25. Sculpted shell mask, Mamora Bay period.

either by scratching their surfaces, applying a red or white slip, or in one instance by red-painting a rectilinear design and outlining it with an incised line. There are graceful, deeply incised, pronged stamps (Figure 24, E–G). Plain or perforated disks complete the list of clay artifacts (Figure 24, D). One of the disks is large enough to be the bottom of a bowl.

STONE ARTIFACTS

Like their ancestors, the Mamora Bay period artisans did little stonework. One celt and a single hammerstone were recovered, together with eight grinding stones of rough local material (Figure 24, H–L). Two three-pointers were found. A small one of limestone has a convex base is pointed at one end and stubby at the other. The second example is medium-sized, made of coral limestone, and has a concave base with a longitudinal groove in the center. Both ends are broken off (Figure 24, M, N).

SHELL ARTIFACTS

Conch shell (*Strombus gigas*) was still the preferred material for making celts and ornaments (Figure 24, O–V). Four celts were found in Excavation 3, together with a hammer, a chisel and a spatula.

There are a number of olive shells, three of them perforated for use as pendants, and two rectangular pieces of conch shell, one of which is drilled. Rounding out the collection is a small, beautifully made conch shell mask with a sculpted face (Figure 25). It measures 4 cm by 5 cm.

CHAPTER FOUR

Radiocarbon
Measurements

Materials and Methods

The charcoal recovered from the Indian Creek site in 1973 consisted predominantly of bits and pieces scattered through the midden refuse. It was bagged by section and level so that each sample could be used to date the assemblage of artifacts found within its excavation unit. Twenty-nine samples were processed in the six excavations (Table 1; see also Davis 1988).

The first 13 samples are from assemblages deposited during the Indian Creek period (Table 1). In his preliminary report on the Indian Creek research, Rouse rejected the two oldest dates, obtained from samples I-7830 and I-7842, because they were 800 years earlier than any other Ceramic Age dates in the West Indies. He also discarded the final date, obtained from sample I-7353, because it overlapped the range of dates for the Mill Reef period. This left 10 valid dates for the Indian Creek period, from I-7980 to I-7352. They indicate that the Indian Creek period lasted from ca. A.D. 1 to A.D. 600.

Since the median values for the dates from Excavation 1 were all earlier than the median values for the dates from the Indian Creek components of Excavations 5 and 6 (Table 1, column 5), Rouse divided the period into two parts. He assigned the Excavation 1 assemblages to an Indian Creek 1 subperiod and the Excavation 5 and 6 assemblages to Indian Creek 2 (Rouse 1976).

Analysis

Our detailed analysis of the Indian Creek collections has revealed no chronologically significant differences between the artifacts from the two subperiods. The relatively minor differences between the two are better explained socially rather than chronologically. The Indian Creek period components of Middens 5 and 6, in the eastern part of the ring of middens, have yielded better made and more artistic artifacts than those in the contemporaneous Middens 1 through 4 in the western part of the site (Figure 3). This difference continues throughout the subsequent Mill Reef period. During both periods the families living in the eastern sector would appear to have

TABLE 1. Radiocarbon dates for the Indian Creek site.

Sample no.	Excavation no.	Section /Level	Reported values B.P.	Median uncalibrated value
The Indian Creek period				
I-7830	1	A1-3	2785 ± 80	835 B.C.
I-7842	1	A2-3	2785 ± 80	835 B.C.
I-7980	1	A4-2	1915 ± 80	35 A.D.
I-7981	1	A4-3	1855 ± 80	95 A.D.
I-7979	1	A3-2	1990 ± 80	160 A.D.
I-7855	6	P3-5	1765 ± 80	185 A.D.
I-7838	6	P2-6	1750 ± 80	200 A.D.
I-7837	6	P3-4	1715 ± 80	235 A.D.
I-7854	6	P2-3	1670 ± 80	280 A.D.
I-7355	5	I2-6	1505 ± 85	445 A.D.
I-7356	5	I2-6	1505 ± 85	445 A.D.
I-7352	5	I1-6	1440 ± 85	510 A.D.
I-7353	5	I1-5	1230 ± 85	720 A.D.
The Mill Reef period				
I-7834	4	G3-5	1265 ± 80	685 A.D.
I-7846	4	G2-4	1140 ± 80	810 A.D.
I-7984	2	C3-5	1124 ± 80	825 A.D.
I-7983	2	C3-3	1110 ± 80	840 A.D.
I-7354	5	I1-4	1100 ± 85	850 A.D.
I-7357	5	I2-4	1080 ± 85	870 A.D.
I-7836	6	P3-2	1070 ± 80	880 A.D.
I-7982	2	C3-2	1070 ± 80	880 A.D.
I-7844	2	C1-2	1000 ± 90	950 A.D.
I-7831	2	C4-3	785 ± 80	1165 A.D.
I-7843	2	C4-2	645 ± 80	1305 A.D.
The Mamora Bay period				
I-7833	4	G4-3	1895 ± 80	55 A.D.
I-7845	4	G1-2	1020 ± 80	930 A.D.
I-7847	5	I1-3	900 ± 90	1050 A.D.
I-7832	3	E4-2	855 ± 80	1095 A.D.
I-7835	5	I1-2	845 ± 80	1105 A.D.

been more affluent and perhaps of higher status than the families in the western sector. The leading families in the eastern sector may have chosen to live adjacent to the creek in order to be close to its fresh water. They may also have preferred that locality because it provided easier access to the shore via the creek. We have therefore decided to abandon the distinction between the Indian Creek 1 and 2 subperiods and to replace it with a division between two social groups, elites and commoners.

Several of the Indian Creek period assemblages show evidence of trade from the Barrancoid series of the South American mainland. These assemblages cannot therefore date earlier than A.D. 250, when the Barrancoid peoples are known to have expanded from their homeland in the Orinoco Valley to the northern Guianas and the islands of Trinidad and Tobago; this opened up the possibility of trade with the Saladoid inhabitants of the Windward Islands, Antigua and Nevis at the southern end of the Leeward islands (Rouse 1992:84–5; Fig. 15).

Eleven charcoal samples were processed in an effort to date the upper boundary of the Mill Reef period. The results, listed in Table 1 after the Indian Creek period dates, place that boundary at about A.D. 600.

Unable to find a sharp break in the sequence of dates that could serve as a boundary between the Mill Reef and Mamora Bay periods, Rouse (1976) arbitrarily chose a closing date of A.D. 900. In effect, he rejected the last two sets of Mill Reef dates in our table because their median values overlap those of the subsequent Mamora Bay period. Five charcoal samples were processed in order to date the Mamora Bay period. The first of these, from sample I-7833, had to be discarded because it was 800 years too early. The other four gave a date of A.D. 900–1100 for that period.

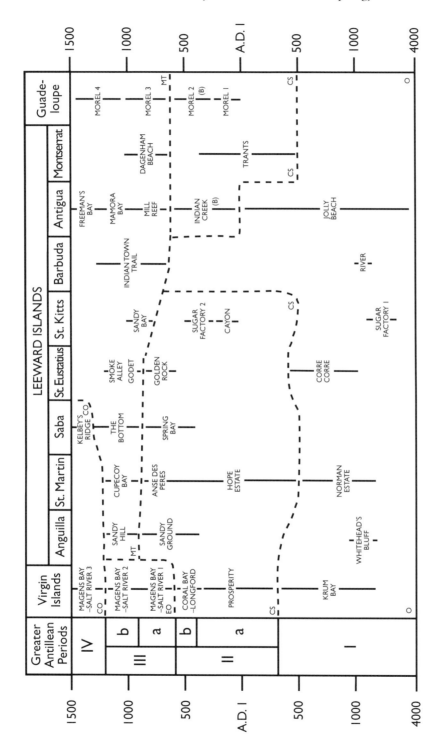

FIGURE 26. Chronology of the Leeward Islands. O, beginning of the Ortoiroid series; CS, beginning of the Cedrosan Saladoid subseries; EO, beginning of the Elenan Ostionoid subseries; CO, beginning of the Chican Ostionoid subseries; MT, beginning of the Mamoran Troumassoid subseries; (B), Barrancoid trade.

CHAPTER FIVE

CONCLUSIONS

Regional Chronology

By the time of the excavations at Indian Creek in 1973, archaeologists had constructed a regional chronology for the Greater Antilles to the north of the Leeward Islands (Rouse 1951) and were about to construct another one for the Windward Islands to the south (Allaire 1975). Rouse envisioned the sequence of periods he planned to establish at Indian Creek as the first in the total number of local sequences needed to set up a third regional chronology, filling the gap between the other two. The subsequent growth of research in the Leeward Islands has enabled him to construct this chronology (Figure 26).

The following discussion of the chronology is taken from a recent progress report on the Indian Creek research (Rouse and Morse 1999, Fig. 11) in which Rouse put together all the known local sequences for the Leeward Islands. The Virgin Islands were added to the left side of his chart and Guadeloupe on the right side to facilitate comparison with the Greater Antillean and the Windward Islands charts, respectively. The Leeward Islands columns were arranged in their proper geographical order except for Barbuda, which he placed alongside Antigua on the assumption that the two were as closely related during prehistoric times as they are today.

The vertical dimension of the chart, from bottom to top, shows the passage of time. The line across its lower part, labeled CS, indicates the time when the Cedrosan Saladoid subseries first appeared on each island. The fact that this line rises gradually from right to left on the chart supports the hypothesis of a Saladoid invasion from South America. The regularity of the line is broken by a sharp rise to ca. A.D. 1 in the Antigua column and to ca. A.D. 600 in the Barbuda column, from which it may be inferred that both islands were bypassed by the first Saladoid settlers.

The upper line in the Guadeloupe and Leeward Islands columns, labeled MT, marks the beginning of the Mamoran Troumassoid subseries. This line slopes gradually upwards from A.D. 600 to 900 as it passes through the Barbuda-to-Anguilla columns, and then falls back abruptly to A.D. 600 on the far side of the Anguilla column. It thus indicates that the Cedrosan Saladoid peoples survived in the central and northern part of the Leewards for 300 years after the Troumassoid peoples had begun to develop in the Windward Islands and the southern Leewards, and after the Ostionoid peoples had emerged to the north in the Virgin Islands and the Greater Antilles. Throughout this period they faced the emergent Elenan Ostionoids across a frontier at the Anegada Passage (Figure 1), as did the Marmoran Troumassoids who followed them.

About A.D. 1200 Chican Ostionoid, a newly evolved subseries of cultures in Hispaniola, spread eastward through Puerto Rico and the Virgin Islands to the frontier at Anegada Passage, replacing the Elenan Ostionoid subseries (Hatt 1932). The Chican Ostionoid peoples subsequently crossed the frontier and established an outpost on Saba Island in the northern Leewards (Hofman and Hoogland 1991:482, 1993:554). This expansion, indicated on the chart by the line labeled CO, does not appear to have affected the inhabitants of Antigua.

Settlement Pattern

The Indian Creek site has survived with relatively little damage thanks to the circumstances of its discovery and its secluded location in an interior valley separated by hills from the European settlements on the coast. Consequently, the site offers a unique opportunity to observe a settlement pattern of the Cedrosan Saladoid and Mamoran Troumassoid peoples.

In his preliminary reports Rouse (1974, 1976, 1978) simply assumed that the space at the site enclosed by the circle of middens was a plaza. The findings of Peter Siegel (1992) at Maisabel in Puerto Rico and of Aad Versteeg and Kees Schinkel (1992) at Golden Rock on St. Eustatius have led us to rethink this assumption. Elsewhere (Rouse and Morse 1999) we have suggested that the inhabitants of the Indian Creek site lived inside the circle of middens with their houses facing a smaller plaza at its center, and that they deposited their refuse behind their houses, thereby forming the circle of middens. This hypothesis is supported by the fact that Midden 2, on the western side of the circle, extends up onto the hillside where the inhabitants are unlikely to have lived (see *Description* in Chapter 2), and that the middens on the eastern side extend down a relatively steep slope towards the creek. The hypothesis is also consistent with the irregular distribution of the periods around the ring, indicating that the inhabitants varied the directions in which they threw their refuse. Excavation just inside the ring may be expected to reveal traces of houses; its center should be sterile. The presumed open space at the center of the ring may have been a forerunner of the plazas lined with upright stone slabs that appear in the later sites of the Greater Antilles, such as Caguanas in Puerto Rico (Alegría 1983). It is likewise comparable to the clearings in the centers of present day villages in Guyana and Belize on the mainland (Lovén 1935:99).

ANIMAL REMAINS FROM THE INDIAN CREEK SITE, ANTIGUA

Introduction

The faunal remains that are the subject of this report were excavated from three units from the Indian Creek site not previously studied. These faunal assemblages are associated with archaeological remains from three successive periods of occupation (Figure 26): Excavation 1 corresponds to the late Saladoid, Indian Creek period (A.D. 1–600); Excavation 2 is the early Troumassoid, Mill Reef period (A.D. 600–900); and Excavation 3 dates to the middle Troumassoid, Marmora Bay period (A.D. 900–1100). This allows assessment of changes in animal use through time. Other research has shown major changes in resource use between the Saladoid and following occupations. This will be possible to examine with the faunal assemblages from Indian Creek; however, two of the three samples are small, so any comparisons must be made with caution. The large faunal assemblage from Excavation 2 can be compared with other faunal samples to characterize Troumassoid animal exploitation on Antigua.

The prehistoric uses of animals have been more intensively studied on Antigua than on many other Lesser Antillean islands. Faunal assemblages have been reported from the Mill Reef site and from three additional excavation units at Indian Creek (Wing et al. 1968; Jones 1985). Study of faunal remains from Blackman's Point, a Troumassoid site on the north coast, was made in cooperation with research conducted by Bruce Nodine. The faunal assemblages from Indian Creek, Mill Reef and Blackman's Point are similar in many respects and allow a comparison of the focus of animal exploitation on Antigua.

Materials and Methods

The proveniences from which faunal remains were identified are the largest samples from each excavation. They include: Excavation 1, Sections A3 and A4, Levels 0.00 to 0.50; Excavation 2, Sections C1, C2 and C3, Levels 0.25 through 0.75; and Excavation 3, Sections E2 and E4, Levels 0.00 through 0.50 (Figure 5). Two worked bones are described from Excavation 2, Section C4, Level 0.50 to 0.75. Only the sample from Excavation 2 is large enough (867 identified specimens) to be considered representative of species typically found in sites on this island. Samples from Excavations 1 and 3 are much smaller (129 and 105 identified specimens, respectively). Because of the great difference in the sample sizes between Excavation 2 and Excavations 1 and 3 caution must be exercised in comparing them with one another and with other faunal assemblages.

The material reported here includes 46 vertebrate species represented by 998 vertebrate fragments and three crabs species represented by 103 crab fragments (Tables 2–5). The remains were recovered with coarse one-quarter inch gauge screen, the same screen size used in the recovery of faunal material from other parts of the Indian Creek site and from Mill Reef and Nonsuch Bay. When finer mesh sieves are used a component of small-sized fishes are recovered from most West Indian sites. Except for the Blackman's Point site these are missing from the sites on Antigua.

Standard zooarchaeological techniques were used to identify and quantify these remains. All identifications were made to the lowest possible taxon by comparing archaeological specimens with reference skeletons in the collections of the Florida Museum of Natural History. Basic quantification is a count of the numbers of specimens identified to each taxon. An estimate of minimum numbers of individuals (MNI) is based on the most abundant unique element, augmented by specimens that differ in size. For example, three small right dentaries and one large left dentary of one species would indicate four MNI.

Standard measurements are a guide to the size of the animals represented (Table 6). The measurements of the width of the occipital condyles and femur head depth of mammals and the width of the vertebral centrum correlate allometrically with body weight, and by extension to the potential amount of meat each could have provided (Wing and Brown 1979). The allometric formulas are derived from modern comparative material with data on live body weight. Three allometric formulas are used here to estimate the sizes of the animals used. They are:

$$\text{Log } y = 3.2659(\text{Log } x) - 0.9421 \quad r^2 = 0.96$$

where y = body weight (gms) and x = breadth (mm) of occipital condyles of terrestrial mammals;

$$\text{Log } y = 2.5569(\text{Log } x) + 0.8671 \quad r^2 = 0.96$$

where y = body weight (gms) and x = depth (mm) of the femur head of terrestrial mammals;

$$\text{Log } y = 2.047(\text{Log } x) + 1.162 \quad r^2 = 0.72$$

where y = body weight (gms) and x = anterior width (mm) of vertebral centra of bony fishes.

These estimates are particularly pertinent for domestic animals like the dog and managed animals like the agouti because of the variability in size due to the human control of breeding. Size estimates are also important for fishes by providing infor-

TABLE 2. Species list of animals identified from the Indian Creek site. Fish common names follow *American Fisheries Society Special Publication No. 20,* and crab common names follow *American Fisheries Society Special Publication No. 17.*

Scientific name	Common name	Remarks
Mammals (Woods 1989)		
Muridae		
Oryzomyine (tribe)	rice rats	extinct
Caviidae		
Cavia porcellus	guinea pig	prehispanic introduction
Dasyproctidae		
Dasyprocta leporina	agouti	prehispanic introduction
Canidae		
Canis familiaris	dog	prehispanic introduction
Birds (Bond 1985)		
Procellariidae		
Puffinus lherminieri	Audubon's shearwater	oceanic, nests in crevices usually during early spring
Pelecanidae		
Pelecanus sp.	pelican	coastal
Sulidae		
Sula sp.	booby	open sea and coastal
Ardeidae		
Ardea herodias	great blue heron	
Nyctanassa violacea	yellow-crowned night heron	swamps
Anatidae		
Anas sp.	duck	swamps/lagoons
Rallidae		
Porphyrula martinica	purple gallinule	dense aquatic growth
Columbidae		
Columba sp.	pigeon	woodland
Zenaidura sp.	dove	open lowlands
Strigidae		
indet. owl		
Reptiles (Schwartz and Henderson 1991)		
Cheloniidae		
Chelonia mydas	green sea turtle	marine
Iguanidae		
Iguana iguana	iguana	terrestrial

Continued

TABLE 2 CONTINUED.

Scientific name	Common name	Remarks
Cartilaginous fishes (Randall 1983)		
Lamniformes		
Orectolobidae		
Ginglymostoma cirratum	nurse shark	reef
indet. shark	shark	marine
Rajiformes		
indet. ray	ray	marine
Bony fishes		
Elopidae		
Megalops atlanticus	tarpon	inshore/estuarine
Albulidae		
Albula vulpes	bonefish	inshore/estuarine
Belonidae		
cf. *Strongylura* spp.	needlefish	surface water, inshore
Holocentridae		
Holocentrus spp.	squirrelfish	reef carnivore
Centropomidae		
Centropomus spp.	snook	inshore/estuarine near mangroves
Serranidae		
Epinephelus spp.	grouper	reef
Mycteroperca spp.	grouper	reef
Carangidae		
Caranx cf. *hippos*	crevalle jack	young in shallow brackish-water
C. latus	horse-eye crevally	in- or offshore reefs
Lutjanidae		
Lutjanus spp.	snapper	reef/estuarine /mangroves
Haemulidae		
Anisotremus sp.	porkfish	reef carnivore
Haemulon spp.	grunt	reef carnivore
Sparidae		
Calamus sp.	pluma	inshore/grassy areas
Pomacanthidae		
Pomacanthus sp.	angelfish	reef omnivore

Continued

TABLE 2 CONTINUED.

Scientific name	Common name	Remarks
Labridae		
Bodianus rufus	Spanish hogfish	reef carnivore
Halichoeres radiatus	pudding wife	reef carnivore
Halichoeres sp.	wrasse	reef carnivore
Scaridae		
Scarus spp.	parrotfish	reef herbivore
Sparisoma viride	stoplight parrotfish	reef herbivore
Sparisoma spp.	parrotfish	reef herbivore
Sphyraena		
Sphyraena spp.	barracuda	pelagic, reef, inshore
Acanthuridae		
Acanthurus spp.	surgeonfish	reef herbivore
Scombridae		
cf. *Auxis* spp.	frigate mackerel	pelagic
cf. *Euthynnus* spp.	little tunny	pelagic
Balistidae		
Balistes spp.	triggerfish	reef carnivore
Melichthys niger	black durgon	reef carnivore
Diodontidae		
Diodon spp.	porcupinefish	reef carnivore
Land crabs (Walcott 1988)		
Coenobitidae		
Coenobita clypeatus	land hermit crab	
Gecarcinidae	land crabs	

TABLE 3. Faunal remains from the Indian Creek site. Excavation 1, Sections A3 and A4, Levels 0.00–0.25 and 0.25–0.50.

Taxa	Count	%	MNI	%
Oryzomyine	21	16	7	25
Dasyprocta sp.	1	1	1	4
Canis familiaris	20	16	1	4
Sula sp.	2	2	1	4
Ardea herodias	1	1	1	4
Ardeidae	2	2	1	4
Iguana iguana	3	2	1	4
Cheloniidae	40	31	1	4
Carangidae	2	2	1	4
Lutjanus sp.	2	2	1	4
Lachnolaimus maximus	1	1	1	4
Labridae	1	1	0	0
Scarus sp.	3	2	2	7
Scombridae, Tunini	1	1	1	4
Diodon sp.	1	1	1	4
Gecarcinidae	28	22	7	25
Total	129		28	

mation necessary for interpretation of the fishing location and technology.

Comparisons of the faunal remains from the three excavations are made in three ways. Basic data are the summaries of the faunal assemblages (Tables 3–5). These summaries include a count of identified specimens and an estimate of MNI with the percentage of each. The faunas can be grouped according to class: mammals, birds, reptiles, fishes and crabs. For a comparison that stresses the focus of exploitation, species can also be grouped according to the broad habitats in which they are usually found: endemic terrestrial, introduced tame or domestic, inshore estuarine, reef or pelagic animals (Table 7). Grouped according to these categories, the assemblages can be compared using a similarity index (Krebs 1989:304). The index totals the lowest percentage of representation within each category for pairs of sites and is calculated as follows:

$$P = \Sigma \text{ minimum } (p_{1i} \, p_{2i})$$

where P = percentage similarity between samples 1 and 2,
p_{1i} = percentage of species $_i$ in community sample 1,
p_{2i} = percentage of species $_i$ in community sample 2.

This is a simple yet effective way of comparing faunal assemblages. The percentage similarity indices for vertebrates grouped by habitat are compared from each excavation at Indian Creek, and between Excavation 2 and the faunal assemblages at both Mill Reef and at Blackman's Point (Table 8). The faunal material from Excavation 2 is compared with the other sites because it has an adequate sample and was occupied at approximately the same time as these sites.

Results

The faunal assemblages from the three excavations are similar in many respects (Tables 3–5). The most abundant terrestrial vertebrate in each excavation is the endemic rice rat (tribe Oryzomyini, probably the genus *Megalomys*). The rice rats on Antigua were relatively large with an estimated weight of 406 gm, based on the average femur depth of 4.8 mm. West Indian rice rats are being reviewed by David Steadman and Michael Carlton. When this revision is complete the species designation can be assigned and the relationship between the extinct rice rats and others in the West Indies will be better understood. In addition to the rice rats, parrotfishes (Scaridae) and land crabs (Gecarcinidae) are abundant in all excavations. Other animals present in intermediate abundance are sea turtles (Cheloniidae), snook (Centropomidae), grouper (Serranidae), grunt (Haemulidae) and tuna (Scombridae).

Other represented animals, of particular interest from the standpoint of human management, are dogs (*Canis familiaris*), guinea pigs (*Cavia porcellus*) and agouti (*Dasyprocta* sp.). Both the dog and the guinea pig were domestic and brought to Antigua by prehispanic island colonists from South America. The agouti, a large tropical American rodent, is used by people wherever they occur together. The dog remains include a large portion of one skeleton from Excavation 1: left and right mandibles, the basioccipital region of the skull, left humerus, left and right ulna, three radius fragments, left and right innominate, right femur, left and right tibia, one thoracic vertebra, two lumbar vertebrae, one rib and two metatarsal bones. Adult dentition is in place and the skeletal elements are fused, indicating an adult individual. The femur is burned. Despite this one burned element such a complete representation of one individual in Excavation 1 suggests that this is part of a burial. This dog is estimated to have weighed 10.6 kg, based on the 33.2 mm width of the occipital condyles. Two worked bones, a left humerus and a right femur, are associated with Excavation 2 (Section C4, Level 0.50–0.75). A single metacarpus was recovered from Excavation 3. The single guinea pig bone, a right mandible, was recovered from Excavation 2. The estimated weight of the agouti is 1.8 kg, based on femur depth measurements of 8.65 mm. Agouti remains are associated with each excavation although they are not abundant in any.

The worked dog bones from Excavation 2 are similarly modified with diagonally cut shafts resulting in a pointed artifact (Figure 20). The left humerus includes the proximal end with a shaft cut from the lateral side and terminating in a point on the medial side about two-thirds of the distance down the shaft. The cut is smooth and

TABLE 4. Faunal remains from the Indian Creek site. Excavation 2, Sections C1 through C3, Levels 0.25–0.50 and 0.50–0.75.

Taxa	Count	%	MNI	%
Brachyphylla cavernarium	9	1	4	2
Oryzomyine	137	16	26	11
Cavia porcellus	1	0	1	0
Dasyprocta leporina	38	4	10	4
Pelecanus sp.	1	0	1	0
Puffinus lherminieri	25	3	10	4
Anas sp.	1	0	1	0
Rallidae cf. *Porphyrula* sp.	1	0	1	0
Rallidae	2	0	1	0
cf. *Columba inornata*	1	0	1	0
Zenaidura sp.	2	0	2	1
Columbidae	17	2	5	2
indet. owl	1	0	1	0
indet. bird	3	0	0	0
Iguana iguana	42	5	10	4
indet. lizard	1	0	1	0
Chelonia mydas	6	1	1	0
Cheloniidae	15	2	3	1
Ginglymostoma cirratum	1	0	1	0
indet. shark	1	0	1	0
indet. ray	1	0	1	0
Megalops atlanticus	12	1	4	2
Albula vulpes	1	0	1	0
Belonidae cf. *Stronglura* sp.	3	0	2	1
Belonidae	5	1	4	2
Holocentrus sp.	1	0	1	0
Centropomus sp.	4	0	4	2
Epinephelus sp.	41	5	9	4
Mycteroperca sp.	8	1	4	2
Serranidae	16	2	0	0
Caranx cf. *hippos*	7	1	4	2
Caranx latus	11	1	4	2

Continued

Table 4 continued.

Taxa	Count	%	MNI	%
Carangidae	7	1	0	0
Lutjanus sp.	6	1	3	1
Anisotremus sp.	2	0	2	1
Haemulon sp.	20	2	12	5
Calamus sp.	4	0	2	1
cf. *Pomacanthus* sp.	2	0	1	0
Sphyraena sp.	6	1	4	2
Bodianus rufus	2	0	1	0
Halichoeres radiatus	3	0	2	1
Halichoeres sp.	1	0	1	0
Lachnolaimus maximus	7	1	4	2
Scarus coelestinus	29	3	6	3
Scarus sp.	23	3	10	4
Sparisoma viride	34	4	11	5
Sparisoma sp.	6	1	2	1
Acanthurus sp.	73	8	14	6
Scombridae cf. *Auxis* sp.	4	0	1	0
Scombridae cf. *Euthynnus* sp.	3	0	2	1
Scombridae	68	8	9	4
Balistes sp.	6	1	4	2
Melichthys sp.	1	0	1	0
Diodon sp.	91	10	7	3
Gecarcinidae	42	5	11	5
Coenobita clypeatus	9	1	3	1
indet. marine crab	3	0	3	1
Total	867		235	

TABLE 5. Faunal remains from the Indian Creek site. Excavation 3, Sections E2 and E4, Levels 0.00–0.25 and 0.25–0.50.

Taxa	Count	%	MNI	%
Oryzomyine	17	16	6	18
Dasyprocta sp.	2	2	1	3
Canis familiaris	1	1	1	3
Puffinus lherminieri	4	4	1	3
Nyctanassa violacea	4	4	1	3
Iguana iguana	1	1	1	3
indet. lizard	5	5	1	3
Cheloniidae	7	7	2	6
indet. ray	1	1	1	3
Megalops atlanticus	2	2	1	3
Centropomus sp.	5	5	2	6
Epinephelus sp.	2	2	1	3
Caranx sp.	1	1	1	3
Sphyraena sp.	2	2	1	3
Searus sp.	3	3	2	6
Sparisoma viride	4	4	2	6
Scaridae	2	2	0	0
Acanthurus sp.	1	1	1	3
Scombridae	19	18	1	3
Diodon sp.	1	1	1	3
Gecarcinidae	20	19	5	15
cf. *Menippe* sp.	1	1	1	3
Total		105		34

the proximal articulation is flattened. The right femur includes the distal end with a cut starting on the posterior side and ending in a point on the anterior side about three-quarters of the way up the shaft towards the proximal end. The point is smooth and the shaft is polished. The distal end is flattened but abraded rather than smoothly ground. These specimens come from at least one fully adult individual comparable in size to the specimens in Excavation 1. These tools were probably used for piercing something soft. The pointed end and the shaft of the femur are polished; with magnification fine striations along the long axis of the specimen can be seen. A deposit on the surface of the humerus does not allow observation of such details.

These worked dog bone specimens are associated with a faunal assemblage typical of the rest of the excavation although it was not analyzed in detail. The fauna includes rice rats, agouti, pigeon (Columbidae), two unidentified birds, iguana (Iguanidae), sea turtle, grouper, jack (Carangidae), snapper (Lutjanidae), barracuda (Sphyraenidae), wrasse (Labridae), two genera of parrotfishes (*Scarus* and *Sparisoma*), surgeonfishes (Acanthuridae), tuna, land hermit crab (Coenobitidae) and land crab. The faunal assemblage does not indicate a difference in this provenience from others in Excavation 2 that might explain why both of these tools were found together in this unit.

The faunal assemblage, when subdivided according to the habitats in which the represented animals are most frequently found, allows an evaluation of the most productive sources of animal resources. The key habitats are terrestrial zones and coral reefs. This evaluation focuses on vertebrates and crabs but does not include mollusks, which are also very important in most West Indian sites. Important components of the terrestrial group are the rice rats, pigeons and land crabs. Included in this group is Audubon's shearwater (*Puffinus lherminieri*), an oceanic bird that nests in breeding colonies in burrows or rock crevices on islands, usually during early spring. I presume that the shearwaters were caught on the nest, although this cannot be substantiated by the presence of identified bones of immature animals or medullary bone typical of laying females. Reef dwelling fishes include squirrelfishes (Holocentridae), grouper, jacks, snappers, grunts, wrasses, parrotfishes and surgeonfishes. The estimated weight of surgeonfishes is 360 gm, based on the average vertebral width of 4.8 mm. Estimated weights of grouper and jack are 2.6 and 1 kg, respectively, based on three vertebral measurements (12.7 mm and 7.9 mm, the average of two measurements). Many of these fishes also feed over seagrass meadows and in inshore estuarine waters; however, they are all families that are typically included in catches from reef zones.

Inshore and pelagic fishes are not abundant in terms of MNI, but do have easily recognizable vertebrae and thus their sizes can be estimated. Tarpon (*Megalops atlanticus*) prefer estuaries, shallow waters and mangrove flats. The specimens represented in Excavation 2 are estimated to have weighed 3.6 kg, based on the average width of the vertebrae. The pelagic tunas are likely to be either the genus *Auxis* or *Euthynnus*. The estimated weight of those represented in Excavations 2 and 3 are 2 kg and 1.8 kg, based on the average widths of the vertebrae of 11.1 mm and 10.4 mm, respectively.

The percentage similarity comparisons between the three excavation samples and the faunal assemblages from Mill Reef and Blackman's Point show great similarity, with indices between 81 and 90, except in the comparison between Excavations 1 and 2 at Indian Creek, which has an index of 73. The differences between the Saladoid sample (Excavation 1) and the later samples at Indian Creek are accentuated when crabs are added to the faunal assemblage. Samples from Excavations 1 and 2 are the least similar, with an index of 67, while Excavations 2 and 3 are the most similar, with an index of 80. The samples from Excavations 1 and 3, with an index of 78, are almost as similar as those between Excavations 2 and 3. What accounts for this is the relatively

TABLE 6. Measurements of skeletal elements of key species. All measurements in mm.

Measurement	Excavation 1	Excavation 2	Excavation 3
Oryzomyine			
Megalomys sp.			
lower cheek tooth row	9.1	9: 9.1: 9.4: 9.4: 9.4: 9.5: 9.6: 9.6: 9.6: 9.6: 9.7: 9.7: 10: 10: 10: 10.1: 10.2: 10.7	
upper cheek tooth row		9: 9: 9.2	
femur total length		44.7: 45.8: 46.9: 50.9	
femur length from head		44.4: 45.2: 48.3	
greatest depth of femur head	4.8: 4.9	4.4: 4.4: 4.4: 4.6: 4.6: 4.6: 4.6: 4.6: 4.6: 4.7: 4.7: 4.7: 4.7: 4.8: 4.9: 4.9: 4.9: 5: 5.1: 5.1: 5.2: 5.2: 5.2: 5.2: 5.3: 5.4	4.8: 5: 5: 5.1: 5.4
Dasyprocta leporina			
lower cheek tooth row		18.3: 18.8: 19.8: 21	
upper cheek tooth row		15.7	
greatest depth of femur head	8.7	8.6	
Canis familiaris			
greatest breadth of occipital condyles	33.2		
lower molar row	31.7		
lower premolar row	35		
lower P1–M3	65		
Cheloniidae			
carapace thickness	5.3: 5.9: 6.1	3.9: 6.9	9
Ginglymostoma cirratum			
vertebral width		30.8	
Megalops atlanticus			
vertebral width		13.2: 13.8: 14: 14.9: 4.9: 15.2: 17	17.8
Belonidae			
vertebral width		6.5	
Centropomus sp.			
vertebral width		9.9: 12: 13.9: 14	13.7

Continued

TABLE 6 CONTINUED.

Measurement	Excavation 1	Excavation 2	Excavation 3
Epinephelus sp.			
vertebral width		12.7	
Caranx cf. *hippos*			
vertebral width		10.2: 11.8	
Caranx latus			
vertebral width		7.7: 8.1	
Carangidae			
vertebral width		8.3: 10.8: 11.1: 13.2	10.2
Sphyraena sp.			
vertebral width		15.8: 16.8	17.6
Acanthurus sp.			
vertebral width		3.6: 3.6: 3.8: 4: 4.2: 4.2: 4.2: 4.3: 4.4: 4.5: 4.5: 4.5: 4.5: 4.6: 4.6: 4.6: 4.7: 4.7: 4.8: 4.9: 4.9: 5.1: 5.1: 5.1: 5.3: 5.6: 5.6: 5.8: 6.2: 6.2: 7.1	4.5
Scombridae			
vertebral width	12	6.7: 7.4: 7.6: 7.6: 8: 8.2: 8.7: 8.8: 9.1: 9.1: 9.6: 10: 10: 10.1: 10.2: 10.2: 10.2: 10.3: 10.3: 10.4: 10.5: 10.6: 10.6: 10.7: 10.8: 11: 11.1: 11.2: 11.8: 11.8: 11.8: 11.8: 11.9: 12: 12: 12.5: 12.7: 12.8: 13: 13.1: 13.1: 13.5: 13.8: 14: 14: 15: 15.2: 16.3	9.2: 9.6: 9.8: 9.8: 9.8: 10.4: 10.4: 10.4: 10.5: 10.9: 10.9: 11: 11.1: 11.4
Gecarcinidae			
mandibular height		10.2: 10.9	

TABLE 7. Comparison of the vertebrate faunal assemblages from the Indian Creek, Mill Reef and Blackman's Point sites distributed among five habitat groups, based on MNI.

Habitat	Indian Creek						Mill Reef	Blackman's Point
	Excavation 1		Excavation 2		Excavation 3			
	MNI	%	MNI	%	MNI	%	% MNI	% MNI
Endemic terrestrial	11	52	64	29	10	36	29	25
Introduced	2	9	11	5	2	7	2	3
Inshore-estuarine	1	5	24	11	6	21	3	11
Reef	6	29	108	49	9	32	64	58
Pelagic	1	5	12	6	1	4	3	2
Total	21	100	219	100	28	100	N = 869	N = 89

greater abundance of terrestrial animals and the lower abundance of reef fishes in the samples from Excavations 1 and 3 compared with Excavation 2, although the samples from Excavations 2 and 3 are more similar than Excavation 2 is to Excavation 1.

Discussion

The animal remains from these excavations provide clues to human uses of wild and domesticated resources and how this has changed through time. The changes that can be seen at Indian Creek and that have been noted elsewhere are more in degree of exploitation intensity rather than change in the resource base. For example, most of the same species are present in each sample; even land crabs, so abundant in Saladoid deposits, are present throughout the occupation at Indian Creek. Rice rats are most abundantly represented in the Saladoid (Excavation 1), decline in relative abundance in the following Mill Reef period (Excavation 2), and then rebound in the latest Marmora Bay period (Excavation 3), but not to Saladoid abundance. Jones (1985), studying other materials from Indian Creek, also documents a late period increase in rice rats: "[T]here may have been greater exploitation [of rice rats] early and late with a trough between A.D. 900–1000" (Jones 1985:524). We have also found this to be a trend in some Virgin Island and northern Leeward Island sites, and significant at Trunk Bay/Cinnamon Bay on St. Thomas and at the Kelbey's Ridge site on Saba (Wing and Wing, unpublished data, 1997). The reason for this shift might be an intensification of horticulture and a corresponding improvement in environmental conditions promoting expansion of the rice rat population, an hypothesis that needs to be tested with archaeobotanical studies.

In respect to the relative abundance of terrestrial and coral reef animals, the sample from the Marmora Bay period is intermediate between the Saladoid and Mill Reef samples. A relative increase in the representation of inshore estuarine animals

TABLE 8. Percentage similarity indices of the vertebrates and of vertebrates and crabs typically found in the habitats as subdivided in Table 5 are presented below. Further comparisons of vertebrates only are made between Excavation 2 at Indian Creek and both Mill Reef and Blackman's Point. These are based on MNI.

Sites or excavations compared	Percentage similarity index
Vertebrates only	
Excavations 1 and 2 at Indian Creek	73
Excavations 1 and 3 at Indian Creek	81
Excavations 2 and 3 at Indian Creek	81
Excavation 2 at Indian Creek and Mill Reef	86
Excavation 2 at Indian Creek and Blackman's Point	90
Mill Reef and Blackman's Point	90
Vertebrates and crabs	
Excavations 1 and 2 at Indian Creek	67
Excavations 1 and 3 at Indian Creek	78
Excavations 2 and 3 at Indian Creek	80

is evident in the faunal sequence from Saladoid to Marmora Bay. In the Marmora Bay sample inshore estuarine species such as tarpon and snook constitute 21% of the fauna, rivaling reef species in relative abundance in that period. Evidence for over-exploitation may be a shift in relative abundance from territorial carnivorous fishes to herbivorous ones and a decline in their sizes (Wing et al. 1968; Wing and Wing, unpublished data, 1997). Though we do not have evidence for such changes in reef species, the intensification of fishing in inshore estuarine waters may also reflect less productive reef populations.

Domestic and captive animals are always important from the standpoint of human management of resources. If indeed the marine resources were under stress— and this issue must be viewed with caution because of the small sample sizes—then managed resources might be intensified. However, we have not seen this in any sites where overexploitation can be clearly documented, nor is it apparent at Indian Creek.

Even though one of the dog bones was burned, the fact that paired elements of a large part of the dog skeleton are present in the Saladoid sample suggests that this animal was buried rather than eaten. Most dog skeletal remains are found in burials in the West Indies despite the report by Las Casas that they were eaten (Sauer 1966:59). Dogs may, of course, have been eaten as a consequence of the disruption in the lives of the Taino resulting from the European colonization of the Caribbean, and they were eaten in some regions of the circum-Caribbean mainland based on docu-mentary and archaeological evidence. Dogs were believed to have taken an active part in hunting (Lovén 1933:433–34). Dog bones were worked, as were teeth in other parts of the West Indies (Rímoli 1977). The choice to use dog bones and teeth may have been simply that dogs provided the largest bones and canine teeth of island mammals.

The other domesticated animal found in the prehispanic West Indies is the guinea pig, called *cori.* They are known by a similar name, *cuy,* in the Andes where they were domesticated and used for food and ritual. Guinea pigs have a long tradition as animals offered in sacrifice and used in medical diagnosis and treatment. Early accounts indicate that they were eaten on Hispaniola (Sauer 1966:59). Archaeological finds in north central Puerto Rico suggest they were an important part of the prehispanic diet on parts of the island. However, in eastern Puerto Rico, Vieques Island, Antigua and Curaçao such finds are consistently from late prehispanic deposits and are represented by only a few identifiable fragments. Guinea pig remains are associated with both the Indian Creek and Mill Reef sites. Despite study of large faunal samples from the Virgin and Leeward Islands, their remains have not been identified from other islands. This suggests that other than on Hispaniola (Rímoli 1976) and central Puerto Rico guinea pigs were widely used but not abundant. The distribution suggests further that there may have been some special trade connection between Antigua and the Greater Antilles, specifically Puerto Rico. The sparcity of remains in food refuse may indicate that they were used for other purposes; possibly some of the same uses associated with them in the Andes traveled along with their name.

The other managed animal is the agouti, which is found throughout the Lesser Antilles but is rare in all sites. Its rarity among midden refuse may either be because these animals were not regularly used for food or were not easily maintained. Although guinea pig remains are found on both the Greater and Lesser Antilles, with the exception of Vieques Island so far agouti remains are only associated with Lesser Antillean sites. Agouti remains are too rare in sites on Antigua to reveal changes resulting from human management and transport throughout the islands.

In summary, the faunal remains from Indian Creek support other archaeological evidence concerning uses of animals during Ceramic Age occupations on Antigua. Fishing on the reefs was clearly a focus of the food quest. The diminished use of rice rats in the Mill Reef period, followed by intensification of their use in the Marmora Bay period, agrees with Jones' (1985) study of animals at Indian Creek. The possibility that this may be associated with changes in the environment caused by humans, such as increased horticulture, land clearing and larger areas of secondary growth, warrants further investigation. Guinea pigs suggest an association with the islands to the west and the continuation of some of the traditional uses of this animal, at the very least the adoption of a form of its Andean name. Sequences of faunal assemblages from other Leeward Island sites indicate the stress of overexploitation of animal resources. The dynamic changes apparent at Indian Creek may in part be driven by a decline in resources and greater management of the environment and the plants and animals in it.

Elizabeth S. Wing
Florida Museum of Natural History
Gainesville, Florida

REFERENCES

ALEGRÍA, RICARDO E.
1983.   *Ball Courts and Ceremonial Plazas in the West Indies.* New Haven: Yale University Publications in Anthropology No. 79. 185 pp.

ALLAIRE, LOUIS.
1973.   *Vers une préhistoire des Petites Antilles.* Font St. Jacques, Ste. Marie, Martinique: Centre de Recherches Caraïbes, Université de Montréal. 156 pp.
1994.   *Historic Carib Site Discovered!* Winnipeg: University of Manitoba, St. Vincent Archaeological Project Newsletter. 3 pp.

BOND, J.
1985.   *Birds of the West Indies.* Boston: Houghton Mifflin Co. 256 pp.

CRUXENT, JOSÉ M. AND IRVING ROUSE.
1958–9.   *An Archeological Chronology of Venezuela.* 2 vols. Washington, D.C.: Pan American Union, Social Science Monographs No. 6. 277 pp.

DAVIS, DAVE D.
1988.   Calibration of the ceramic period chronology for Antigua, West Indies. *Southeastern Archaeology* 7(1):52–59.

DAVIS, WILLIAM MORRIS.
1926.   *The Lesser Antilles.* New York: American Geographical Society, Map of Hispanic America, Publication No. 2. 207 pp.

FLANNIGAN, MRS.
1844.   *Antigua and the Antiguans.* 2 vols. London.

HARRIS, DAVID R.
1965.   *Plants, Animals, and Man in the Outer Leeward Islands, West Indies.* Berkeley: University of California Press. 184 pp.

HATT, GUDMUND.
1924.   Archaeology of the Virgin Islands. In: *Proceedings of the Twenty-first International Congress of Americanists,* pt. 1. The Hague. pp. 29–42.
1932.   *Notes on the Archaeology of Santo Domingo.* Copenhagen: Saertryk af Geografisk Tidsskrift 35. 24 pp.

HOFMAN, CORRINE AND MENNO HOOGLAND
1991.   The later prehistory of Saba, Netherlands Antilles: The settlement site of Kelby's Ridge (1300–1450 A.D.). In: E.N. Ayubi and J.B. Haviser, editors. *Proceedings of the Thirteenth International Congress for Caribbean Archaeology;* 1989; Curaçao, Netherlands Antilles. Curaçao: Reports of the Archaeological and Anthropological Institute of the Netherlands Antilles, no. 9, pt. 1. pp. 477–492.
1993.   Ceramic developments on Saba, N.A. (1350–1450 A.D.). In: Alessandra Cummins and Philippa King, editors. *Proceedings of the Fourteenth Congress of the International Association for Caribbean Archaeology;* 1991; St. Ann's Garrison, Barbados. Barbados: Barbados Museum and Historical Society. pp. 550–560.

JONES, ALICK R.

  1980a.   Animal food and human population at Indian Creek, Antigua. In: Suzanne M.
           Lewenstein, editor. *Proceedings of the Eighth International Congress for the Study of
           Pre-Columbian Cultures of the Lesser Antilles*; 1979; St. Kitt's. Tempe: Arizona State
           University Anthropological Research Papers No. 22. pp. 264–273.

  1980b.   A report on two types of modification to gastropod and mollusc shells from
           Indian Creek, Antigua. *Journal of the Virgin Island Archaeological Society*
           10:31–40.

  1985.   Dietary change and human population at Indian Creek, Antigua. *American
           Antiquity* 9:31–40.

LOVÉN, SVEN.

  1935.   *Origins of the Tainan Culture, West Indies.* Göteborg, Sweden: Elanders
           Boktryteceri Aktiebolag. 696 pp.

MARTIN-KAYE, P. H. A.

  1959.   *Reports on the Geology of the Leeward and British Virgin Islands.* St. Lucia: Voice
           Publishing Co. 117 pp.

MITCHELL, CARLETON.

  1971.   *Isles of the Caribbees.* Rev. and enl. ed. Washington, D.C.: National Geographic
           Society, Special Publications Division. 208 pp.

MORISON, SAMUEL ELIOT.

  1942.   *Admiral of the Ocean Sea: A Life of Christopher Columbus.* 2 vols. Boston: Little,
           Brown and Company. 858 pp.

MORSE, BIRGIT FABER.

  1997.   The Salt River site, St. Croix at the time of the encounter. In: Samuel M.
           Wilson, editor. *The Indigenous People of the Caribbean.* Gainesville: University
           Press of Florida. pp. 36–45.

MORSE, BIRGIT FABER AND IRVING ROUSE.

  1999.   The Indian Creek period: A late Saladoid manifestation on the island of
           Antigua. In: Gerard Richard, editor. *Proceedings of the Sixteenth Congress for
           Caribbean Archaeology*; 1995 July 24–28; Basse Terre, Guadeloupe. In press.

MULTER, H. G., M. P. WEISS AND DESMOND NICHOLSON.

  1986.   *Antigua: Reefs, Rocks and Highroads of History.* St. John's, Antigua: Leeward
           Islands Science Associates, Contribution 1. 143 pp.

OLSEN, FRED.

  1974.   *Indian Creek: Arawak Site on Antigua, West Indies, 1973 Excavation by Yale
           University and the Antigua Archeological Society.* Norman: University of
           Oklahoma Press. 58 pp.

PETERSEN, JAMES B.

  1996.   Archaeology of Trants, Montserrat, pt. 3, Chronological and settlement data.
           Annals of the Carnegie Museum 65(4):323-361.

PETERSEN, JAMES B. AND DAVID R. WATTERS.

  1999.   Pyroclastic, storm-surge and Saladoid villager deposit: the archeological and
           geological stratigraphy of the Trants site, Montserrat. In: Gerard Richard,
           editor. *Proceedings of the Sixteenth International Congress for Caribbean
           Archaeology*; 1995 July 24–28; Basse Terre, Guadeloupe. In press.

RANDALL, J.E.

1983.   *Caribbean Reef Fishes.* New Jersey: T. F. H. Publications, Inc. 350 pp.

RÍMOLI, R. O.

1976.   Roedores fosiles de la Hispaniola. *Universidad Central del Este, Serie Científica* 3:5–93.

1977.   Nuevas citas para mamiferos precolombinos en la Hispaniola. *Cuadernos del Cendía* 259(5):1–15.

ROBINS, C. RICHARD, REEVES M. BAILEY, CARL E. BOND, JAMES R. BROOKER,
ERNEST A. LACHNER, ROBERT N. LEA AND W. B. SCOTT.

1991.   *Common and Scientific Names of Fishes from the United States and Canada.* Bethesda, Maryland: American Fisheries Society Special Publication No. 20. 183 pp.

ROUSE, IRVING.

1951.   Areas and periods of culture in the Greater Antilles. *Southwestern Journal of Anthropology* 7(3):248–265.

1964.   Prehistory of the West Indies. *Science* 144(3618):499–513.

1974.   The Indian Creek excavations. In: Ripley P. Bullen, editor. *Proceedings of the Fifth International Congress for the Study of Pre-Columbian Cultures of the Lesser Antilles*; 1973 July 22–28; Antigua. Gainesville, Florida: Florida Museum of Natural History. pp. 166–176.

1976.   The Saladoid sequence on Antigua and its aftermath. In: Ripley P. Bullen, editor. *Proceedings of the Sixth International Congress for the the Study of Pre-Columbian Cultures of the Lesser Antilles*; 1975 July 6–12; Pointe a Pitre, Guadeloupe. Gainesville, Florida: Société d'Histoire de la Guadeluope. pp. 335–341.

1978.   Cultural development on Antigua: A progress report. In: *Actas del XLI Congreso Internacional de Américanistas, Mexico*; 1974 September 2–7; Mexico City. Mexico City: Congreso Internacional de Américanistas. 3:701–709.

1992.   *The Tainos: Rise and Decline of the Indians Who Greeted Columbus.* New Haven: Yale University Press. 211 pp.

ROUSE, IRVING AND BIRGIT FABER MORSE.

1999.   The Mill Reef period: Local development on the island of Antigua. In: *Proceedings of the Sixteenth International Congress for Caribbean Archaeology*; 1995 July 24–28; Basse Terre, Guadeloupe. In press.

ROUSE, IRVING, BIRGIT FABER MORSE AND DESMOND NICHOLSON.

1995.   Excavations at Freeman's Bay, Antigua. In: Ricardo E. Alegría and Miguel Rodríguez, editors. *Proceedings of the Fifteenth International Congress for Caribbean Archaeology;* 1993; San Juan, Puerto Rico. San Juan: Centro de Estudios Avanzados de Puerto Rico y el Caribe. pp. 445–457.

SAUER, C. O.

1966.   *The Early Spanish Main.* Berkeley and Los Angeles: University of California Press. 306 pp.

SCHWARTZ, A. AND R. W. HENDERSON.

1991.   *Amphibians and Reptiles of the West Indies.* Gainesville: University Press of Florida. 720 pp.

SIEGEL, PETER E.

    1992.   *Ideology, Power, and Social Complexity in Prehistoric Puerto Rico* [doctoral dissertation]. Binghamton: State University of New York. 806 pp. Available from University Microfilms, Ann Arbor, Michigan.

VERSTEEG, AAD H. AND KLEES SCHINKEL, EDITORS.

    1992.   *The Archaeology of St. Eustacius: The Golden Rock Site.* St. Eustacius: Publication of the St. Eustatius Historical Foundation No. 2. 334 pp. (also Amsterdam: Publication of the Foundation for Scientific Research in the Caribbean Region No. 131).

VESCELIUS, GARY S.

    1952.   *The Cultural Chronology of St. Croix* [B.A. thesis]. New Haven: Yale University. Available from Division of Anthropology, Peabody Museum of Natural History.

WALCOTT, THOMAS G.

    1988.   Ecology. In: W. W. Burggren and R. B. McMahon, editors. *Biology of the Land Crabs.* Cambridge: Cambridge University Press. pp. 55–96.

WEISS, MALCOM P.

    1994.   Oligocene limestones of Antigua, West Indies: Neptune succeeds Vulcan. *Caribbean Journal of Science* 30(1–2):1–29.

WILLIAMS, AUSTIN B., LAWRENCE G. ABELE, DARRYL L. FELDER, HORTON H. HOBBS JR., RAYMOND B. MANNING, PATSY A. MCLAUGHLIN, ISABEL PÉREZ FARFANTE.

    1989.   *Common and Scientific Names of Aquatic Invertebrates of the United States and Canada: Decapod Crustaceans.* Bethesda, Maryland: American Fisheries Society Special Publication No. 17. 77 pp.

WING, E. S. AND A. B. BROWN.

    1979.   *Paleonutrition.* New York: Academic Press. 202 pp.

WING, E. S., C. A. HOFFMAN JR. AND C. E. RAY.

    1968.   Vertebrate remains from Indian sites on Antigua, West Indies. *Caribbean Journal of Science* 8(3–4):123–139.

WOODS, C. A., EDITOR

    1989.   *Biogeography of the West Indies: Past, Present, and Future.* Gainesville, Florida: Sandhill Crane Press. 878 pp.